The Cold-Bath Treatment Of Typhoid Fever

Francis Everard Hare

THE COLD-BATH TREATMENT
OF TYPHOID FEVER

THE EXPERIENCE OF A CONSECUTIVE SERIES OF NINETEEN HUNDRED AND TWO CASES TREATED AT THE BRISBANE HOSPITAL

By

F. E. HARE, M.D.

LATE RESIDENT MEDICAL OFFICER, BRISBANE (GENERAL) HOSPITAL, QUEENSLAND

WITH ILLUSTRATIONS

London

MACMILLAN AND CO., LIMITED

NEW YORK: THE MACMILLAN COMPANY

1898

RICHARD CLAY & SONS, LIMITED,
LONDON & BUNGAY.

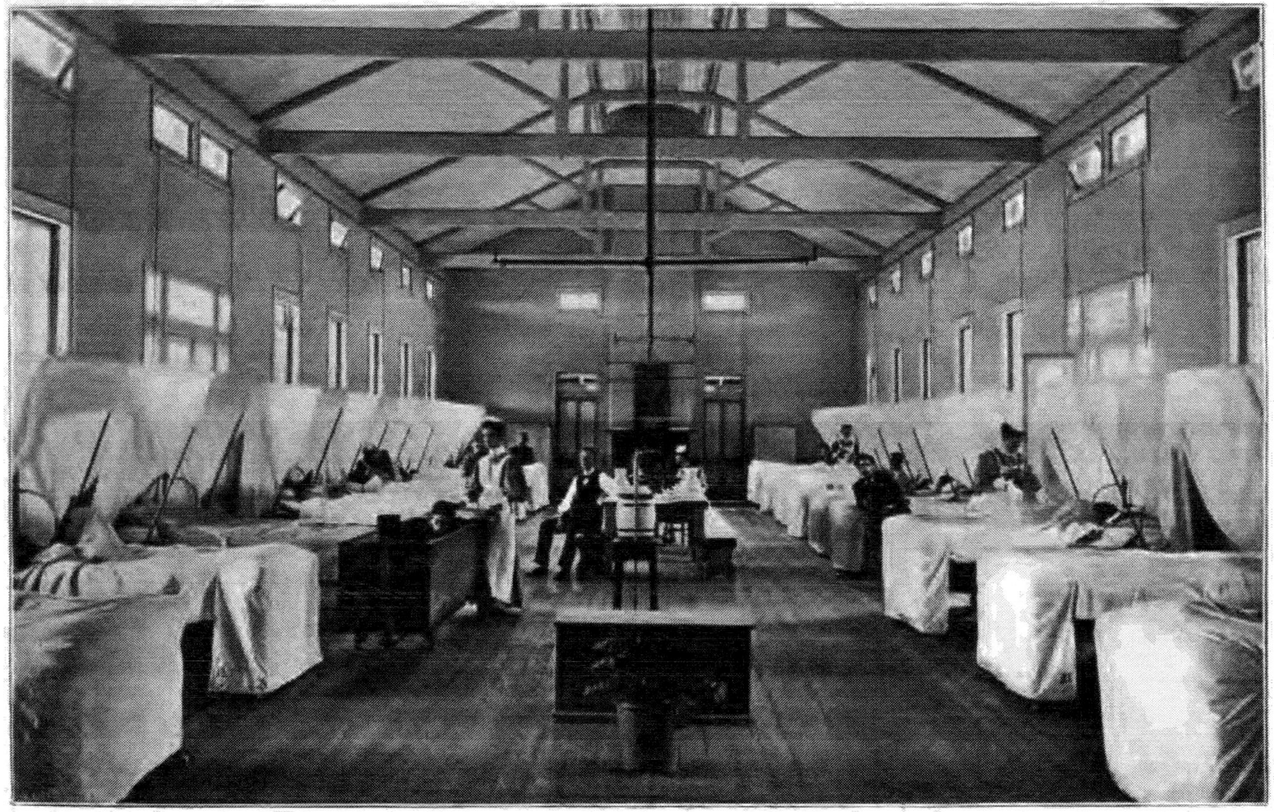

MALE FEVER-WARD, BRISBANE HOSPITAL.

Frontispiece.

PREFACE

MEDICAL literature threatens to grow to such unwieldy dimensions, that the first duty of every author should be to offer the profession some satisfactory excuse for seeking to add to its bulk. I have been induced to attempt this sketch of the Cold-bath Treatment of Typhoid Fever, as carried out at the Brisbane Hospital, by the following considerations—

(1) There is not, so far as I am aware, any single modern work upon the subject in the English language. Such information as is obtainable is scattered through the pages of the various medical journals, or is contained in hospital-reports not readily accessible.

(2) The treatment in recent years has made great and steady advances in various parts of the world. In America it is in use at the Pennsylvania and German Hospitals, Philadelphia; at the Royal Victoria Hospital, Montreal; and at the Johns Hopkins Hospital, Baltimore. In Australia, at

several of the country hospitals of Queensland, at the Alfred Hospital, Melbourne, and at the Prince Alfred Hospital, Sydney, it is now on its trial. In spite of this there still exists a large amount of serious misconception on the subject. Even amongst those who are inclined to accept the statistical evidence on its behalf, and to believe in the life-saving value of the treatment, it is too often regarded as burdensome in practice, if not altogether impracticable. The inertia of the profession in England in this respect is exemplified in the following paragraph taken from the *British Medical Journal* for the current year. "The practice is in the *experimental* stage [*the italics are mine*]; it is very much disliked by patients and their friends; it needs very close supervision by the medical man and a picked staff of experienced nurses; and finally, if carried out in all cases, costly and cumbrous apparatus is required." It will be shown that each count of this indictment is incorrect.

(3) The Brisbane Hospital has always, on account of immigration and other causes, had a large fever-department. Outside Germany and after Lyons, it was the first hospital of any size which definitely adopted Brand's system and carried it out systematically in all cases. Consequently there is on hand an abundance of clinical material, more than sufficient indeed definitely to prove the value of

the treatment without having recourse to statistics from elsewhere.

The matter contained in this book is mainly a record of personal observations made in the Fever-wards and Post-mortem room of the Brisbane Hospital. These observations are for the most part extensions and confirmations of those of Brand, Liebermeister, Jürgensen, Cayley, Coupland, Glenard, Tripier and Bouveret, Osler, J. C. Wilson, and others, and no claim for originality is made except in regard to a few minor and comparatively unimportant details. I have also consulted the writings of Winternitz, who has done so much to place the subject of Hydrotherapeutics upon a rational basis.

I have not attempted a complete discussion of the treatment of typhoid; my aim has been simply to describe the nature of the treatment called for in the ordinary types of the fever which form the vast bulk of hospital cases. The only qualification which I claim for the task is a sufficient personal experience of the disease, extending over upwards of 2000 cases.

I have departed somewhat from the usual plan of arrangement. After defining the general characters of the clinical material, I have described the routine treatment as applied to an ordinary uncomplicated case, together with the necessary practical details; next, the influence exerted by this practice upon the symptoms, course, duration, mortality, and prognosis of the disease; and lastly, the contra-indications and the additional therapeutic procedures called for at times and in special instances.

I have dwelt especially upon the practical details of the system, for these have not, I think, hitherto received sufficient attention. There is no doubt that the supposed mechanical difficulties of systematic cold-bathing have caused many to shrink from trying the treatment in the first instance.

The statistics contained in the chapter on Mortality constitute to my mind an irrefutable argument in favour of cold-bathing. For those, however, who are still inclined to withhold their assent, but one loophole remains, so far as I can see. This is a doubt, quite natural, but usually of course unexpressed, as to the good faith of the statistician. With the object of anticipating this objection, in part at any rate, all the documents, such as charts, clinical histories, and post-mortem records of the cases, have been filed at the Brisbane Hospital, where they can be consulted by those who are sufficiently interested in the subject.

My special thanks are due to Dr E. Sandford Jackson, the Medical Superintendent, and to the Honorary Staff of the Brisbane Hospital for the efficient and consistent manner in which they have carried out the treatment in recent years, and for their kindness in placing the records at my disposal; to Dr A. Jeffries Turner, of the Sick Children's Hospital, Brisbane, for valuable help in revising the original MS; and to Dr Donald MacAlister of Cambridge for kindly consenting to see the book through the press.

CONTENTS

CHAPTER I

CHAPTER II

CHAPTER III

CHAPTER IV

CHAPTER V

CHAPTER VI

LIST OF ILLUSTRATIONS

THE COLD-BATH TREATMENT OF TYPHOID FEVER

CHAPTER I

INTRODUCTORY

General Considerations

To the late Dr Brand of Stettin is undoubtedly due the present position of the Cold-bath Treatment of Typhoid. Imbued with the theory that in the high temperature itself lay the main source of danger, he proceeded to formulate a plan of external antipyresis which should, with occasional minor modifications, be applicable to the great majority of cases.

The plan he finally adopted, which is now widely known as " Brand's rule," may be briefly stated. The patient's temperature is taken in the rectum every three hours day and night, and on each occasion that it attains or exceeds 102·2° F. a full-length bath is administered, of a temperature about

B

68° F. and a duration approximately of fifteen minutes.

The rule in all its details was the outcome of actual experience. The rectal temperature of 102·2° F. (39° C.) was chosen as the bathing-point, because it was found that above this the symptoms of pyrexia usually became urgent; the interval of three hours was prescribed, because it was usually not until the expiration of this period that the temperature regained its previous height; the temperature of the bath-water was laid down, because 68° F. was found on the average to be sufficiently low.

Although Brand's rule was formulated with the specific object of keeping the temperature from rising above a certain point, subsequent experience has amply demonstrated that cold-bathing acts in many other ways, all more or less conducive to the welfare of the typhoid patient. And, although the present writer is still inclined to attribute a large share of the benefits received to the reduction of the temperature *per se*, there has recently been a tendency, even amongst those who are the strongest supporters of the system, to regard the merely antipyretic action as of but secondary importance.

Whatever view be adopted, there is no question that, of all the symptoms of typhoid, the temperature merits the most earnest consideration, if only for the fact that it gives the *earliest* warning of danger. High temperature, if not in itself a source of danger, certainly indicates severity in the disease, and thereby emphasises the urgent necessity for systematic refrigeration. Hostile critics are fond of saying that the temperature is of little moment provided the pulse remains satisfactory. This is of course true, but nothing is more certain than that, if the temperature remains continuously high, sooner or later the pulse will fail, and by that time the opportunity for successful treatment will in all probability have passed. Thus it comes about that the *temperature* still remains the chief index for treatment amongst the advocates of cold-bathing in all parts of the world.

No complete theory as to the action of the treatment is at present available. It appears to act primarily more upon the manifestations of the morbid process than upon the process itself, although undoubtedly the latter is in this way indirectly controlled. The effects upon the various symptoms of the fever are dealt with individually in the succeeding chapters.

"The treatment stands by itself as a definite procedure, not to be confounded with the treatment of enteric fever by graduated baths, the cold pack, cold affusions, sponging, continuous immersions, or other hydrotherapeutic measures. It is especially to be looked upon as a method entirely distinct and

3

different from any *merely* antipyretic treatment"
(*J. C. Wilson*).

From the expectant method it differs fundament-
ally. Expectancy relies upon the fact that the
great majority of cases pursue their course towards
recovery without serious interruption; its practice
consists in attention to diet, hygiene, and good
nursing. Active interference begins only when
special or abnormal symptoms arise.

Brand's treatment is based upon the following
considerations: (1) That in any case of prolonged
pyrexia, certain unfavourable symptoms and complications are liable to arise; (2) That while we
know that these occur in a fairly constant proportion of cases, yet it is impossible to foresee them in
any given case; (3) That it is usually possible to
prevent them by systematic bathing; but (4) That
when once they have arisen, active interference is
too often of no avail.

Brand's treatment then is to be regarded as
essentially a prophylactic against the consequences
of protracted pyrexia. Hence, *to obtain the greatest
possible benefit from it, it is above all things necessary that it be commenced at the earliest possible
period of the fever, before signs of danger have
appeared; and in direct proportion as this indication is responded to is the success of the treatment.*

To such an extent is this statement true, that in

4

a series of cases treated boldly and systematically
from an early period of the fever (*i. e.* from the fifth
day) the old clinical picture of typhoid is lost.
Were it not that in every hospital cases continue to
be admitted in the later stages, and that conditions
not infrequently arise which necessitate the suspension of the bathing, it would be easy to fall into
the error of attributing the milder course of the
disease to an alteration in its type, irrespective of
the treatment pursued.

Most of the objections commonly preferred to the
treatment will be dealt with in discussing the influence of cold-bathing upon the symptoms of the
disease. Two however may more conveniently be
referred to here.

The first is the sentimental objection. Preju-
diced writers have not hesitated to describe the
treatment as *barbarous* and *brutal*. It is inconceivable that any one who had had personal experience of it could have used such terms. Osler indeed, who goes so far in its support as to say that
nothing should be allowed to stand in the way of
its adoption until some more life-saving method is
available, describes it as a harsh and unpleasant
procedure. But the experience of the Brisbane
Hospital is not in accordance with this description.
The sensations connected with the first few baths,
even in timid patients, do not amount to more than

slight discomfort; while the almost immediate relief to *malaise* and febrile oppression which follows the bath renders the patient willing, at times even eager, for its repetition. Allowance must, however, be made for the fact that Brisbane is almost tropical in its climate.

The other objection is the diagnostic difficulty. It is said that early treatment necessitates early diagnosis, and that this is frequently impossible in typhoid. It seems probable that in the future the difficulty will be met by the method of serum-diagnosis, but it must be stated that at no time has any real difficulty arisen here, from the point of view of practical therapeutics. Fortunately there exist no diseases, that are indistinguishable at an early stage from typhoid, in which cold-bathing exercises an injurious influence; all those that are liable to be mistaken for it being actually benefited or at any rate not unfavourably affected thereby. Delay therefore on this account is quite unjustifiable; it is enough for us to recognise the presence of a fever of sufficient intensity, certain well-understood contra-indications being of course kept in mind.

The real argument in favour of Brand's treatment, however, rests upon the results obtained from it. The number of recorded cases is enormous. In the words of Osler, it "has forced its way to recognition by the overwhelming array of figures which can be brought in its favour." J. C. Wilson, of the German Hospital, Philadelphia, says, "As the treatment is systematically carried out as a routine practice, the statistics of various observers in widely-separated countries become available for comparison, and their aggregate is now sufficient to enable us to disregard the variations in the mortality of the diseases in different places, seasons, and epidemics."

Despite all that has been said to the contrary, the subject of typhoid offers special facilities for statistical treatment. The great majority of persons attacked are otherwise healthy youths or adults. The wide variations in respect of severity, course, and duration, which affect the individual, are found to disappear almost completely when a sufficiently long series of cases is viewed in the aggregate. The number and diversity of the complications and of the modes of death, which render the disease itself so treacherous, are not only no hindrance to the application of the statistical method, but they in fact materially assist it. By their aid it is possible to split up a long list of cases into quite natural classes; and thus the statistics, in addition to proving the life-saving value of the treatment, help us to advance inductively some distance towards a true explanation of its mode of action and to define somewhat sharply its limitations.

The want, elsewhere so often experienced, of a

control-list showing the mortality of the untreated disease is in the present instance easily met. For many years the mortality of typhoid has varied but little in the large hospitals of England, the United States, and Australia, and this in spite of the numerous and diverse methods of treatment that have been in vogue at different periods. Therefore it may be assumed that the average mortality-rate, of say from 14 to 17 or 18 per cent., represents simply the result of good nursing, diet, and hygiene.

Clinical and Pathological Material, and Introduction of the Treatment into the Brisbane Hospital

Since most of the matter contained in the succeeding pages is drawn from observations made in the Fever-wards and Post-mortem room of Brisbane Hospital, it will be expedient in the first place to give some account of the clinical material at the writer's disposal, and to describe shortly the exact manner in which the new treatment was introduced.

From May 15, 1882,[1] to December 31, 1886, the treatment in the Brisbane Hospital differed in no essential respect from that which is at present carried out in most of the hospitals of England, America, and the Colonies. Expectancy was in the main relied upon; but cold-sponging was frequently used, and the cold wet-sheet not uncommonly applied

[1] Prior to this date the Hospital-records were incomplete.

in cases with persistent high temperatures. This whole period, which may be termed the " entire expectant period," furnishes a series of 1828 consecutive cases. It will serve as a standard of comparison in certain points only, namely, the general mortality, the sex-mortality, and the mortality of the different age-periods, since these are the only particulars preserved in the Hospital case-books.

During the last seventeen months of this period, however (*i. e.* from August 1, 1885, to December 31, 1886), clinical records of all the cases were kept under my own supervision. The points to which attention was chiefly directed were—the day (third, fourth, etc.) of fever on admission and at the termination of the disease; the number, severity, and date of occurrence of the more important symptoms and complications; the drugs administered; and the immediate (*i. e.* the secondary) cause of death in each fatal case as disclosed by post-mortem examination. This period, which may be termed the " shorter expectant period," furnishes a series of 586 consecutive cases, which are susceptible of moderately minute and accurate analysis. It will therefore be from a comparison of this series with those of the " bath-periods," which follow, that most of our inferences as to the value and mode of action of the cold-bath treatment will be drawn.

9

On January 1, 1887, the bath-treatment was introduced. Usually a new line of treatment is commenced tentatively; cases that are presumed to be most suitable are selected, and the effect on the symptoms and progress of the disease is carefully watched. But many considerations tended to the belief that in the present instance this course was inexpedient. It was fully realised that Brand's treatment was essentially a prophylactic measure directed against the results of protracted pyrexia, and not a directly curative agent in the ordinary sense of the term. Evidently therefore its value was to be gauged in the main *from what it prevented*, and not from any dangers it might counteract when these were already present. But evidence of this nature was manifestly only to be obtained statistically, and could not be gathered from observations on selected cases. Consequently it was decided to avoid the tentative method as tending to fallacy.

The treatment was therefore introduced suddenly on the day specified. January 1 was selected as being the commencement of a new statistical year. Being also in the height of the fever-season, it was thought that any alteration in the aspect of the disease, such as was hoped for from the change, would be thrown into bold relief.

Every case that was admitted on or after that

date was submitted systematically to a course of cold-bathing, very similar in detail to that recommended by Brand. The only exceptions were—(1) a very few patients (practically limited to the first year) who refused to submit to it; (2) cases in which the temperature throughout failed to attain the bathing-point; (3) cases where contra-indicating conditions existed.

The above course has been pursued uninterruptedly down to December 1896, so that there is available for comparison a " bath-period " extending over ten complete years. This period, which may conveniently be termed the " bath-decade," furnishes a series of 1902 consecutive cases.

It is from a comparison between this series and those of the " expectant periods," already defined, that most of our important conclusions as to the value of the treatment,. *e. g.* the reduction in the mortality, will be drawn. But for some, such as the immediate influences exerted upon the symptoms of the disease, I shall have to fall back upon the first three years of the " bath-decade " (*i. e.* from January 1, 1887, to December 31, 1889), during which I was myself in charge of the Fever-wards. This period furnishes a series of 1173 consecutive cases, all the records of which were kept under my own supervision. These records were similar to those made in the " shorter expectant period," but the following additional notes were taken—the duration of each bath and the exact time of its administration; the temperature and the pulse-rate immediately before and half-an-hour after its termination; and the temperature of the bath-water used.

CHAPTER II

THE ROUTINE TREATMENT : PRACTICAL DETAILS

Special Wards

ALL cases are treated in special wards reserved for typhoid. Apart from the danger of infection, this is found to have many practical advantages.

1. The possibility of completely excluding visitors. This is a point of much importance; all who have spent much time in Fever-wards recognise the baneful influence exerted by the visits of friends and relations. These tend to cause in severe cases restlessness and exhaustion, and nearly always occasion a perceptible increase in the evening temperature-rise. The evil is not limited to the patient visited, but is apparent to a less extent in patients occupying adjoining beds.

2. The smuggling of injurious articles of diet can be effectually blocked. The most careful supervision cannot prevent this from happening at times in an ordinary medical ward to which visitors are admitted.

13

3. No difficulty is met with in overcoming the common initial prejudice of patients against cold water in a ward where all alike are submitted to it. So potent is the influence of example that the bath is usually accepted as a matter of course. In the rare instances in which it has been refused on first admission, it has almost invariably been demanded on the following day.

Ventilation

Free ventilation is essential, not only to carry off the products of respiration, etc., always excessive in a Fever-ward, but also to keep the air at the lowest possible temperature. This applies to at least eight months of the year in Queensland. The ward-windows are accordingly kept constantly open, day and night, and absolutely no notice is taken of draughts, except in the case of convalescents.

Coverings

During the summer a single sheet only is allowed, and in winter one thickness of blanket in addition. Night-shirts have been discarded during the continuance of the bathing at all seasons of the year. Their frequent removal and replacement was found to entail much exhaustion. No harm has ever arisen from these apparently stringent regulations, while there can be no doubt that by their means

14

alone a considerable reduction in the average temperature of the patients has been maintained.

One is forced therefore to conclude that the danger of catching cold, which is so greatly dreaded by the public, and which still largely regulates the practice of the profession, has a purely imaginary existence. This is true, however, only so long as the patient's temperature is raised above the normal : during convalescence the danger is a real one, if indeed it is not, as seems probable, somewhat greater than in health. When nothing further is to be gained by refrigeration, the convalescent patient is protected from draughts, has a warm night-shirt, and is allowed to follow his inclinations in the matter of bed-clothes.

Diet

The diet in ordinary cases consists of milk and beef-tea, usually three pints of the former with one or more of the latter *per diem*. In all cases the milk is treated strictly as a food, and is given in regular quantities at regular times. The time for administering nourishment and drinks is of much importance. Iced water is allowed *ad libitum*, and may be given when asked for; usually, however, it is most grateful before or just after immersion, when the temperature is at its highest and the buccal cavity parched and dry. Food, by which is

15

usually meant milk and beef-tea, is, on the other hand, best given about half-an-hour after the termination of the bath, when the temperature-fall is being noted. At this time the temperature is at its lowest, the mouth and tongue are comparatively clean and moist, and the patient is generally at his best. Food consequently is less distasteful at this time, and probably undergoes better digestion.

Beef-tea is usually omitted during the continuance of diarrhœa. While admitting the low value of this article of diet as a food, it has appeared to act as a valuable stimulant, and it is usually much appreciated by patients.

There are of course cases where the ordinary diet of milk and beef-tea is inappropriate, on account of idiosyncrasy or other cause; cases also in which, owing to extreme emaciation, the quantity of nourishment towards the end of the fever requires to be greatly increased; and cases in which considerable modifications in the quality of the food, especially in the direction of predigestion, are imperatively called for. Such cases, however, occur under any treatment, and their management may safely be left to ordinary medical rules. Under systematic cold-bathing they occur with less frequency than under expectant and drug treatment, and generally speaking the dietetic management of cases is much simpler than under the latter.

Alcohol

Great difference of opinion still exists as to the use of alcohol in fever. The indications accepted for its administration at the Brisbane Hospital will be dealt with when we come to consider the temperature and the circulatory symptoms. Here it is necessary to say only that harm has never been observed to accrue from its moderate exhibition in any case, although doubtless in the majority of cases it is not essential. In hospital-practice, therefore, considerations of economy may be allowed to limit its use.

Text-books usually contain a warning as to the effects of alcohol; they state that if its administration is followed by increased temperature and pulse-rate, dry tongue, delirium, etc., it is to be at once suspended. This is doubtless good advice, but the occurrence of such symptoms as an effect of alcohol must be extremely rare. At any rate they were never observed at the Brisbane Hospital during the writer's time.

The form in which the alcohol is given does not seem to be of much importance, provided always it is pure, good of its kind, and acceptable to the patient.

Baths and the Mode of their Administration

Practical details are here of much importance, and have not generally received sufficient attention. The following are the appliances in use in the Brisbane Hospital Fever-wards.

1. *The Baths.*—These are constructed of three-quarter-inch plank lined with galvanised-iron, materials which combine the advantages of lightness, strength, and cheapness. They are rectangular in form, and measure 72 inches in length by 22 wide and 19 deep. When ready for use they should be two-thirds full, and then will be found to contain about 75 gallons. At one end of the bottom is a waste-plug, three inches in diameter. This is better than the ordinary tap, since from its size it saves much time in emptying, and is not liable to injury in moving. The bath is mounted on four wheels ; one pair (the larger) is fixed, the other pair being attached to a revolving under-carriage. From the front of the latter projects a hinged handle for convenience of moving. The best wheels are the patent-tyred trolley-wheels made by Warne and Co. of London ; and the axles should be turned, to ensure silence and smoothness of motion.

2. *The Stretcher.*—This is made of perforated canvas, stretched between two light poles of wood, the extreme ends of which are connected by light

galvanised-iron cross-bars. Its dimensions are such that it fits loosely the bottom of the bath, upon which it rests during the patient's immersion (Fig. 1).

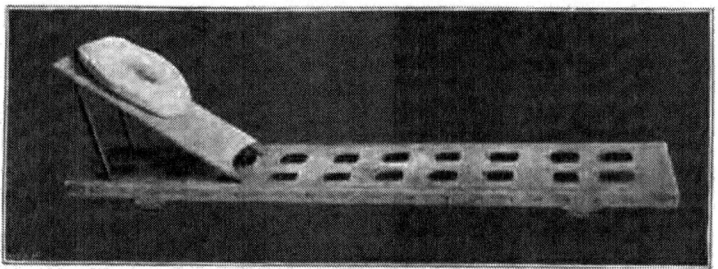

Fig. 1.

The uprights in the figure do not belong to the apparatus. They are introduced simply to support the back-rest in the position it assumes in the bath.

3. *The Back-rest.*—This is a light wooden frame filled in with canvas. It is a little narrower than the Stretcher, so as to rest comfortably within the poles. When in use it acts as an oblique support for the shoulders and head of the patient (Fig. 1).

4. *Circular Water-cushion,* with central diaphragm for the support of the patient's head (Fig. 1). This rests upon the upper part of the Back-rest. An air-cushion is useless for this purpose, as it floats up, and thus raises the head of the patient uncomfortably. A large bath-sponge, placed under the nape of the neck and occiput, makes a good substitute for the Water-cushion.

5. *Piece of board* (30 inches by 10 inches).—
When the bath is to be used, it is wheeled into
position across the end of the bed. There is
nothing to be gained by placing it alongside; indeed
this makes the lifting considerably more difficult
and awkward. Also, it more than doubles the
distance through which the bath has to be moved
between each patient, and correspondingly increases
the disturbance and noise in the ward. By adopt-
ing the transverse position, a whole row of patients
may be bathed in succession, the bath being simply
moved onwards in a straight line.

The patient, otherwise quite naked, is covered
with a small sheet or towel from about the ensiform
cartilage to the knees. His head and neck are then
well sponged with water reduced by means of ice to
about 60° F. The Stretcher is placed diagonally
under the thigh and right leg. On the Stretcher,
at the end nearest the patient's head, but projecting some six or eight inches beyond it, is
placed the Back-rest supporting the Water-cushion
(Fig. 2).

The patient is then raised a few inches from the
bed, the male attendant supporting the head and
shoulders, the nurse lifting the thighs and lower extremities. A slight rotatory movement now places
the patient in position on the Stretcher (Fig. 3).

The whole is then lifted from the bed and gently

FIG. 2.

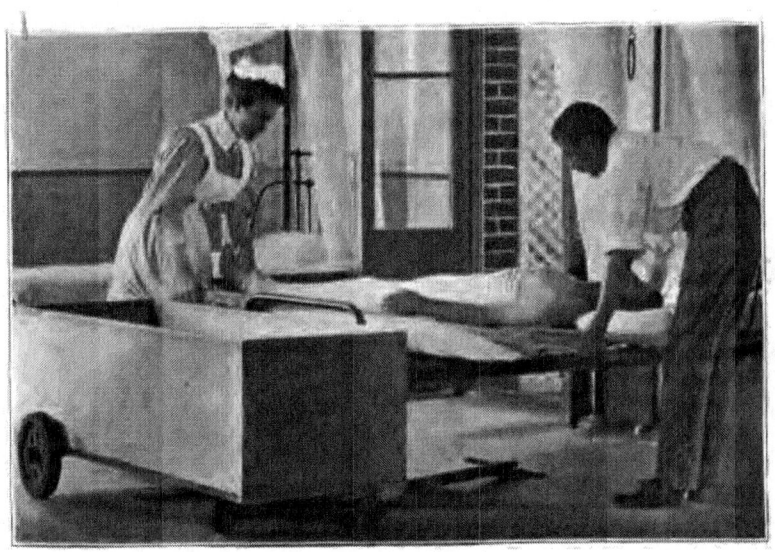

FIG. 3.

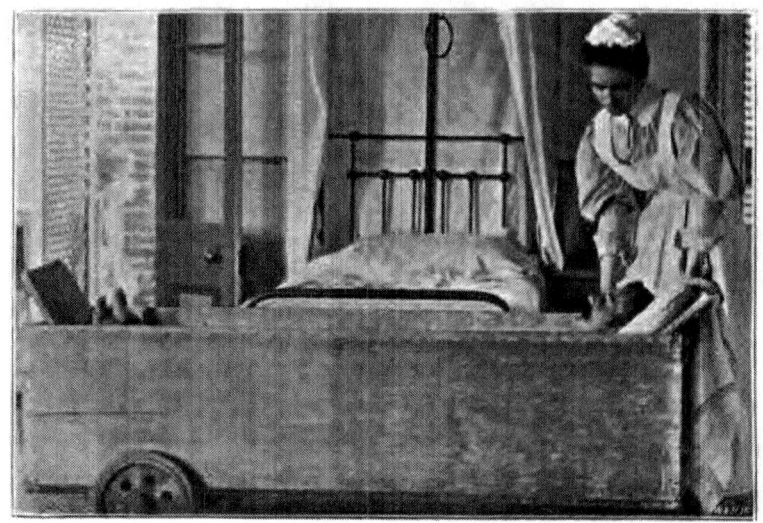

FIG. 4.

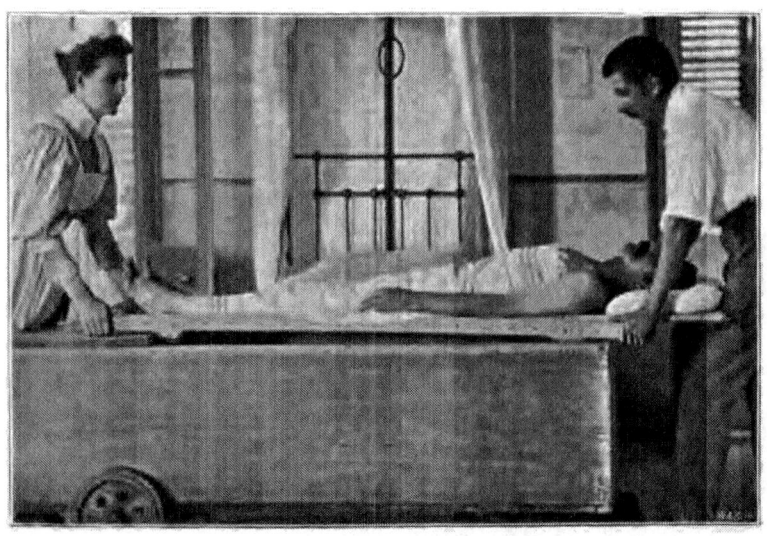

FIG. 5.

lowered into the bath. In the descent the Back-rest, by its projecting end, catches on the end of the bath and gradually comes to assume an oblique position at an angle of about 45°. Against it rest comfortably the head and shoulders of the patient. Usually the foot-end of the Stretcher is now raised somewhat by means of the board. This obviates any tendency on the patient's part to slip forward ; and by keeping the anterior part of the feet out of water, it prevents too severe chilling of the toes (Fig. 4).

At the end of the bath the Stretcher is slowly raised, the back-rest falling gradually into its original horizontal position. The head of the Stretcher is then rested on the corresponding end of the bath, while the board is used to support the foot (Fig. 5).

After remaining about a minute in this position, to drain off the excess of water, the whole is lifted and placed in its original oblique position on the bed (Fig. 3), which is now covered with mackintosh sheeting. Off the Stretcher the attendants lift the patient by reversing the manœuvre which placed him thereon. He is then dried, and, the mackintosh being withdrawn, covered with the bed-clothes according to the season.

The whole procedure can be accomplished in the case of a full-sized adult by one nurse and one male attendant; in the case of a lighter patient by two nurses. In Fever Hospitals, however, where many patients require bathing, the work is too exhausting for women. It is better then to have all the lifting, both in male and female wards, done by male attendants. In the female wards, the patient is of course fully prepared for the bath before the lifters are summoned. In Brisbane, during the great fever-seasons (1887—1890), four wardsmen were set apart for this work, two for day and two for night duty.

Any one who has watched a bath given after the manner described must be convinced that the bathing is effected easily and rapidly, and with the minimum of exertion on the patient's part. Nurses have frequently stated that the administration of a bath is to them less onerous than that of a general cold-sponging.

Many plans of bathing are open to serious objection. To lower a heavy patient into a bath without the assistance of a rigid support is by no means easy; to lift him out is a matter of great difficulty, and is certain to be accompanied by much struggling on his part. Complicated arrangements of frames and pulleys, etc., are tedious to work, and create much unnecessary fuss and noise in the ward. In parts of the Continent the patient is allowed in the first place to step in and out of the bath himself, and is only lifted later on when weakness has become marked. This is essentially bad both in principle and practice. The great advantage attaching to the use of one uniform plan from the commencement is that, long before prostration has become advanced or intestinal ulceration deep, the patient has become educated to avoid all unnecessary exertion during the procedure.

The number of baths necessary, in wards containing only acute cases, is one to about twelve patients; with a smaller number the bathing can hardly be carried on punctually. Thus at the Brisbane Hospital, where the two typhoid wards for acute cases contain forty-eight beds, the four baths during the great fever-seasons were almost constantly in use; and it was often found possible at the height of the season to administer without great difficulty one hundred and fifty and upwards in the course of twenty-four hours.

Preliminary treatment.—On admission, should the patient not have reached the ninth day of the fever, the bowels are freely moved by some un-irritating purgative, usually castor-oil. This is omitted in those cases—not uncommon—in which the patient has already dosed himself with aperients under the impression that he is suffering from a bilious attack.

As an aperient calomel was given in a considerable number of cases, in doses of five grains, this being sometimes repeated on two or three consecutive days. It has been supposed in virtue of its antiseptic action to cause the disease to abort in a certain number of cases, but experience in the Brisbane Hospital did not confirm this. Quite as large a proportion of cases ran an abortive course after castor-oil, or indeed without anything at all.

Calomel too has some decided drawbacks; it not rarely fails to act even in large and repeated doses, while it sometimes causes excessive irritation, starting a diarrhœa to restrain which opiates become necessary.

The advantage of the initial aperient is probably simply to remove the remains of improper and undigested food, usually present in the alimentary canal on admission, and thereby to moderate the severity of the subsequent diarrhœa and other intestinal symptoms. Castor-oil therefore came to be almost exclusively used for this purpose, being prompt and certain in its action, and in every respect absolutely harmless.

Rule for the administration of the baths.—The baths are commenced at once. The rule for their administration is similar to that recommended by Brand, except as regards the temperature of the water. During the greater part of the fever-season in Queensland, it is impossible to obtain water at 68°F.

without great expenditure on ice. Frequently the temperature of the water as it flows from the main is 75° or even 80°; and from economical considerations the use of ice is reserved for cases of intense pyrexia.

The temperature of the patient is taken in the rectum every three hours day and night, and on every occasion that the thermometer registers 102·2° F. or more, a bath is given. The temperature of the bath-water may be anything between 70° and 80°, but more commonly approximates to the former. The duration of the first bath is ten minutes. Half-an-hour after its termination, the temperature of the patient is again taken in the rectum, when the fall should be to 101° or lower.

In the cases where this result is not attained, various modifications in the temperature and duration of the baths are introduced, all of which will receive consideration further on.

The plan of bathing above indicated is pursued systematically throughout the whole course of the fever, until such time as the temperature ceases to rise to 102·2°. The approach of convalescence is seen in the gradually diminishing number of baths, so that usually, for some days before they definitely cease, one or two during the evening are all that have been required.

Care is always taken that the patient is not unnecessarily disturbed. To this end food, stimulants, medicines, etc., are given at intervals of three hours or some multiple of this time, except in the cases, to be afterwards considered, where the baths are given more frequently. In this way the patient remains quite undisturbed during the interval, which in the majority of instances is wholly devoted to sleep.

Before each bath the patient is made to pass water, since if this is omitted, the shock of the immersion will produce an almost irresistible desire to urinate in the bath.

In one other respect the plan of bathing adopted at Brisbane differed somewhat from that of Brand. Brand advises that during the bath the surface of the patient's body should be subjected to constant friction by the attendant. In this way shock is lessened, and Winternitz has pointed out that refrigeration is also much facilitated. In the Brisbane Hospital, at the commencement of the treatment in 1887, the staff was not sufficiently large to allow of one nurse devoting her whole time to one patient during the bath. Choice had to be made therefore between bathing only a certain proportion of the patients and omitting the frictions as a general rule. The latter alternative was selected, on the ground that the value of the whole experiment depended mainly on the number of data obtainable.

Name *E. B.*   Age *32*   Religion *Methodist*

Birthplace *England*
Occupation and Condition *Labourer – Single.*
How long in Colony *3 years.*
Last Residence *Macronan Bridge.*

Admitted *19. 7. 97.*
Discharged *1. 9. 97.*
Disease *Typhoid Fever*
Result *Convalescence*

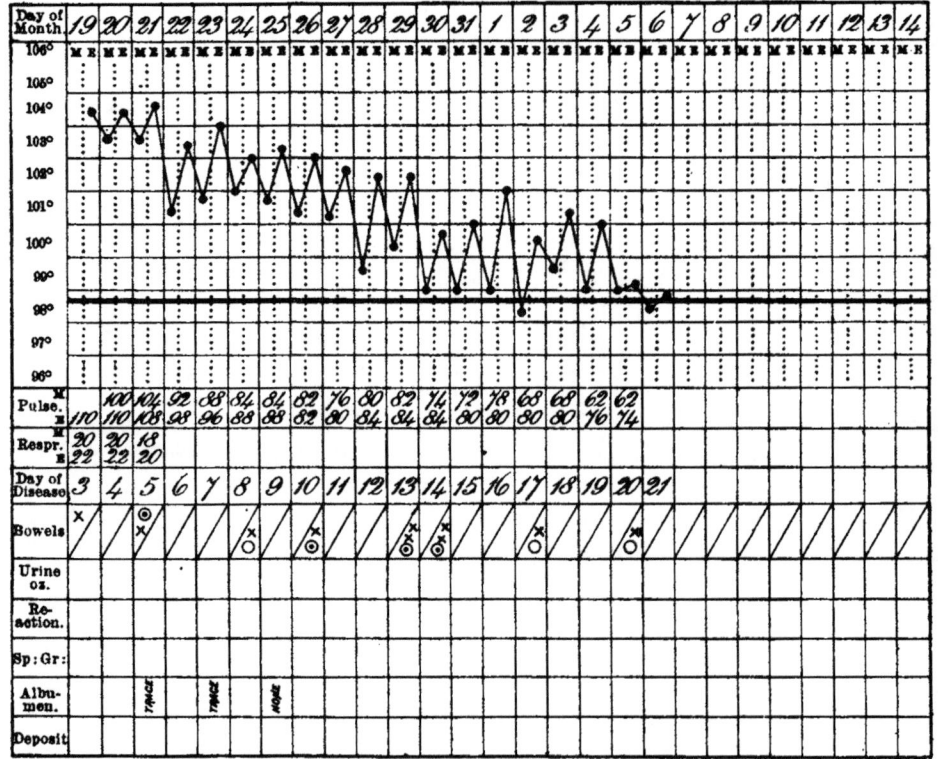

Day of Month	19	20	21	22	23	24	25	26	27	28	29	30	31	1	2	3	4	5	6	7	8	9	10	11	12	13	14
Pulse. M		100	101	92	88	84	84	82	76	80	82	74	72	78	68	68	62	62									
Pulse. E	110	110	108	98	96	88	88	82	80	84	84	84	80	80	80	80	76	74									
Respr. M	20	20	18																								
Respr. E	22	22	20																								
Day of Disease	3	4	5	6	7	8	9	10	11	12	13	14	15	16	17	18	19	20	21								
Bowels	✕		⊙ ✕				✕/○		✕/⊙			✕/○ ✕/⊙			✕/○			✕/○									
Urine oz.																											
Reaction.																											
Sp: Gr:																											
Albumen.			TRACE		TRACE	NONE																					
Deposit																											

History. First complained on August 16th during the afternoon of very severe pain in back of neck and general headache, but did not leave off work until Aug 18th.

On admission: complained of severe general pains, with the usual symptoms of pyrexia.

Aug. 22. This case is evidently not dengue for which it has hitherto been mistaken. Commence bathing at once.

Fig. 6.   Face p.

Frictions were accordingly reserved for special cases, and were applied chiefly to the extremities when these tended to become excessively chilled or painful. That they were omitted in the majority with impunity is probably to be explained by the higher average temperature of the bath-water in Queensland.

Chart and clinical record.—To enable a brief account of the main features of each case to be preserved for compiling statistics, and also to show the effect of treatment day by day, the appended chart has after several modifications been finally selected. It consists of four pages, the first of which contains the ordinary temperature-chart for morning and evening observations, with spaces attached for noting pulse and respiration rates, and the state of the urine and bowels. In filling in the last, a code of signs was found of great convenience, denoting the various kinds of motions passed, enemata administered, etc.

The remaining three pages are ruled in columns for recording the number, duration, and effects of the bath on the temperature and pulse rate, a wide margin being left for notes as to special symptoms, additional points of treatment, etc.

The ordinary chart on the front page is intended to convey some idea of the natural course of the temperature as it would appear if uninterfered with

27

BATH COLUMNS OF THE RECORD.

Date.	Time.	Before.		Bath.	After.		
		Temp.	Pulse.		Temp.	Pulse.	
Aug. 22	11 a.m.	105	92	20 m.	102·8	90	Temp. of water about 70° F.
	2 p.m.	103·4	86	25 m.	102·2	88	
	5 ,,	103·2	96	30 m.	104	92	
	8 ,,	103·4	92	35 m.	101	82	
	11 ,,	103·2	88	30 m.	102·6	80	
,, 23	2 a.m.	102·6	88	30 m.	102	84	
	5 ,,	103·2	84	40 m.	122	88	
	8 ,,	102·2	88	40 m.	100·8	80	
	11 ,,	101·8	84				
	2 p.m.	104	96	45 m.	101·4	79	
	5 ,,	101·8	76				
	8 ,,	104	96	40 m.	102·2	80	
	11 ,,	102·6	84	35 m.	101·8	76	
,, 24	2 a.m.	103	92	20 m.	102	84	Cold compresses to abdomen in the interval between the baths.
	5 ,,	102	86				
	8 ,,	102·6	88	40 m.	101·8	78	
	11 ,,	102·4	88	40 m.	101·8	76	
	2 p.m.	102·6	88	40 m.	100·8	108	
	5 ,,	101·8	108				
	8 ,,	103	88	20 m.	102·4	72	
	11 ,,	102·2	88	25 m.	100·8	82	
,, 25	2 a.m.	102	86				
	5 ,,	102	84				
	8 ,,	101·6	76				Temp. of water to be 78° F. during the night.
	11 ,,	102	76				
	2 p.m.	103·2	88	20 m.	102	84	
	5 ,,	102	84				
	8 ,,	103	84	20 m.	102·2	80	
	11 ,,	102·4	82	25 m.	101·4	80	
,, 26	2 a.m.	101·4	82				
	5 ,,	101·6	84				
	8 ,,	101·6	82				
	11 ,,	101·8	88				
	2 p.m.	102·8	80	25 m.	101·8	76	
	5 ,,	101·8	84				
	8 ,,	101·8	84				
	11 ,,	103	82	Bath refused.			
,, 27	2 a.m.	102	84				
	5 ,,	101·4	80				
	8 ,,	101 2	76				
	11 ,,	101·8	76				
	2 p.m.	102·6	84	20 m.	101·2	76	
	5 ,,	101·8	74				
	8 ,,	102·6	80	20 m.	101·8	50	
	11 ,,	100·8	72				
,, 28	2 a.m.	100	76				
	5 ,,	99·6	80				
	8 ,,	101·2	82				
	11 ,,	100·8	96				
	2 p.m.	102	88				Temp. of water 80° F.
	5 ,,	102·4	84	25 m.	101	70	

P.S. No further bathing required. Improvement in all symptoms set in immediately after the commencement of bathing; the pulse being especially benefited.

by antipyretic measures. In filling it in, therefore, the lowest morning temperature taken at least three hours after the last bath, and the highest evening temperature, are selected out of the numerous thermometric observations on the bathing-record, the pulse and respiration rates being taken at the same time.

From the form of the bathing-record, it is possible to see at a glance the effect of each bath on the temperature and pulse, and to direct thenceforward the amount and kind of refrigeration to be used. Also by entering in the margin any modification in the treatment, drugs, stimulants, etc., opposite the time of their commencement, their effects immediate or otherwise are readily appreciated.

Many of these details may be deemed superfluous; most of the conclusions, however, to be afterwards set down,, depend upon observation, and nothing more detracts from the value of this than a want of uniformity in the method of record.

The amount of personal supervision which it is advisable for the medical attendant to exercise over the actual administration of the baths will vary considerably. In hospital-practice, where many cases of typhoid are treated, it is always possible to have the services of a specially-trained nurse, and then it is rarely necessary for the physician to be present at the bathing in ordinary cases. Perhaps it might be as well to see the patient during his first immersion, though I confess I have long since given up this as a regular practice. It is sufficient as a rule to make one visit daily to each patient, and then to give general instructions as to the treatment to be followed until the following day. Only in exceptional cases is anything further required.

In private practice, however, if no specially-trained nurse is procurable, it will be necessary for the physician to supervise personally the first few baths, and to give detailed instructions concerning them; in fact, some time should be given at the beginning of the case to the careful training of the nurse. But should this be for any reason impossible, I have no hesitation in saying that any dangers that may arise in the course of the bathing, from inexperience on the nurse's part, are inconsiderable when compared with the risk of leaving the temperature to run its course unchecked.

A not uncommon minor objection to the treatment may here be conveniently referred to, namely, that of expense. Our experience at the Brisbane Hospital is that the treatment is distinctly economical, except in the one item of ice. This, however, is the fault of the climate, and would hardly be felt in cooler latitudes. Apart from this, the extra expenses are (1) the initial cost of the bathing-appliances, which need not amount to more than £7 or £8 for each complete set; and (2) some extra male assistance. In the Brisbane Hospital Fever-wards, on the introduction of cold-bathing, two extra wardsmen were found necessary, making four in all. The men worked under the supervision of the charge-nurse, and consequently no special qualifications were required.

These extra expenses were, in our opinion, more than counterbalanced by a considerable saving in other directions. Thus both the drug and alcohol bills were very largely reduced ; and the average stay in hospital was considerably abbreviated.

CHAPTER III

THE INFLUENCE OF THE TREATMENT ON THE SYMPTOMS AND COMPLICATIONS OF THE DISEASE: CONDITIONS WHICH MODIFY IT

Temperature

ORDINARILY the ultimate effect of a cold bath on a fever-patient is a reduction of temperature ; but this result is not a simple one analogous to the cooling of an inanimate body.   Indeed the primary effect of a cold bath, as was long ago pointed out by Liebermeister, is a rise of the temperature of the interior of the body.   After a time, varying widely in different cases and under different circumstances, the internal temperature begins to fall, and this continues for some time after the immersion is over. Various theories were propounded to account for this. The one most generally accepted was that of Lieber-meister, namely, that during the bath, especially at its commencement, there was a great increase in the production of heat.   To explain the beneficial in-fluence of cold-bathing he assumed that this initial

32

increase in the production of heat was followed by a period during which the production of heat was diminished; and that the latter compensated or more than compensated for the former.

Winternitz, however, has shown that there is a fallacy underlying this explanation; and that it consists in under-estimating the influence of the automatic heat-regulating function of the body, the chief factors in which are the cutaneous circulation and the circulation in the subjacent muscular layer. In proof of his contention he has demonstrated that it is possible to prevent the initial rise of the internal temperature that follows immersion, by measures which prevent the contraction of the cutaneous vessels. According to him the sequence of events following immersion is—

(1) A falling temperature of the surface of the body. This causes a reduction of the "heat-tension" or "temperature-gradient" between the skin and the heat-abstracting mediums in contact with it, and thereby a diminution in the rate of heat-loss.

(2) A limitation of the cutaneous circulation, due to vasomotor constriction; and a collateral hyperæmia of the subjacent muscles over the whole body. The former is followed by a diminished loss of heat, the latter prevents too deep and facile penetration by the cold to the deeper organs.

(3) An elevation of the temperature of the

D

muscular layer, recognisable by means of the thermometer in the axilla. This is caused by (*a*) thermal reflex, (*b*) collateral hyperæmia, and (*c*) in all probability an increased heat-production due to the collateral hyperæmia in the tissue under consideration.

(4) Finally, a reduction in the general temperature of the body. This occurs only after the immersion has been continued for some time, and is itself an indication that the automatic heat-regulation of the body has been overcome.

After the patient has been removed from the bath the internal temperature continues to sink for a time. The explanation is simple. During immersion the skin is cooled to a much greater extent than the inner parts, and on removal, therefore, the equalisation of temperature, which has now become possible, necessitates a transference of heat to the periphery.

The facility with which patients part with their fever-heat varies widely according to a number of circumstances. The coldness of the water and the length of immersion have naturally a powerful influence. While it is true that in any given case a bath of lower temperature will have a greater refrigerating effect than one of higher temperature, the duration of the two being equal, yet it is not possible to establish anything like a constant

34

numerical ratio between the temperature of the water and the reduction in the patient's temperature. The reason for this would appear to lie mainly in the varying reaction of the cutaneous circulation to the action of waters of different temperatures ; very cold water causing apparently a proportionally greater constriction of the blood-vessels in the skin, and consequently a greater collateral hyperæmia in the muscular layer.

The duration of immersion is the chief point to consider. The internal temperature never, in any circumstances, commences to fall until immersion has lasted for some time ; in other words, a certain portion of the cooling power of the bath is immediately after immersion used up in overcoming the heat-regulating power of the body ; during the remainder of the immersion the temperature is falling. Nothing but experience in each individual case will determine the duration of immersion necessary to reduce the temperature to the required degree, although, by taking into consideration all the circumstances which will be shown to influence the reducibility of the temperature, a fairly accurate forecast may sometimes be made.

Ceteris paribus, heat-production is proportionate to body-weight; the rapidity of heat-abstraction by cold-bathing is proportionate to body-surface only. Hence weighty subjects part with their heat with great difficulty, and this is especially the case when much subcutaneous adipose tissue exists.

Very muscular people have always been regarded as bad subjects for typhoid. Certainly their temperatures are very difficult to reduce. It is probable that, in their case, in addition to the influence of mere body-weight, the production of heat per unit of mass, occurring mainly in striated muscle, is above the average, and becomes an important factor.

It follows naturally that children part with their fever-heat with extreme facility.

Sex is stated to have some influence, although personally I have never noticed it. According to Liebermeister, women have their temperature less easily reduced than men; but he concludes that this is due simply to the fact that they possess as a rule a better-developed layer of subcutaneous fat.

The time of day has an effect on the reducibility of the temperature. Temperatures of the same height in the same patient are more readily reduced during the night, and especially in the early morning hours, than during the forenoon and afternoon. This is simply due to the natural tendency of the fever to remit and to exacerbate at these times respectively. In other words, a falling temperature is more easily reduced than a rising one; a fact which might have almost been anticipated, but which has been proved experimentally by Lieber-meister.

The reducibility of the temperature also varies according to the type of the fever. As a rule the more this approaches the remittent form, the more easily is it reduced ; while temperatures that show little difference between morning and evening observations are always obstinate. This is true also in a marked degree of the varying types of fever which obtain at different stages in any one case. Towards the end of the first week, and throughout the greater part of the second, the temperature presents only slight morning-remissions in severe cases. It is at this period that the greatest difficulty is met with in refrigeration; while later on, when morning-remissions are becoming marked, a temperature which may be actually higher is found to give way with comparative ease. This increasing reducibility of the temperature reaches its climax in those cases where towards the termination the fever assumes the intermittent type.

In some cases the obstinacy of the temperature in the early stages is quite remarkable. The initial rise of temperature, which immediately succeeds and always attains its greatest elevation shortly after immersion, instead of giving way during the bath persists to such an extent that sometimes the temperature is as high or even higher after the patient has been replaced in bed; and although there is then almost always a fall, it is but slight and transient.

After the febrile temperature has been reduced by the bath, it remains more or less stationary for a time, and then ascends, probably to its previous height or even higher. Tripier and Bouveret divide the temperature-curve following the bath into (1) the period of descent, (2) the stationary period, and (3) the period of ascent. The period of descent, if the bath has been sufficiently prolonged, commences during immersion, but in all cases continues after it is over for at least ten minutes, frequently for half-an-hour or more. The remaining two periods have a duration, generally speaking, which is inversely proportional to that of the period of descent, *i. e.* cases which part with temperature rapidly and easily, recover it but slowly, and *vice versâ*. Consequently all those circumstances already enumerated which render refrigeration difficult and prolonged, assist in shortening both the time that the temperature remains down, and the time it takes to regain its previous height.

Hitherto reference has been made to the effect of a single bath on the temperature. There is, however, an even more important question to decide, namely, What influence, if any, may be exerted on the course of the temperature throughout the case by frequent and systematic bathing? It has been asserted that the object of the treatment is to create a state of "relative apyrexia," *i. e.* to keep the temperature constantly below 102·2° F., a point above which the symptoms of pyrexia become prominent. This, however, I have come to regard as a lofty ideal, which it may be as well to keep in view, but which in the vast majority of cases is either unattainable or unnecessary. It is unattainable in cases of intense fever, in which the temperature after giving way with much difficulty rapidly rises to its previous height. Here, in order to maintain a state of relative apyrexia, it would be necessary to keep the patient almost constantly in the water; so much so, at any rate, that insufficient time would remain for rest and sleep. It is unnecessary in the cases which easily part with their fever-heat and regain it but slowly—the only cases, in fact, in which it is possible.

Nevertheless, in all cases, even the most intense, a very considerable reduction in the average daily temperature is attained. The injurious effect of high temperature depends upon two factors, (1) its height, and (2) its duration. Systematic bathing, if it does nothing else, regularly breaks in upon the continuity of the temperature, and thereby gives the organism frequent periods of relief, the benefits of which are most striking at the time

39

even to the unskilled onlooker. Thus cases which would otherwise present almost a continued type of fever come to rank under the treatment with those that are more or less remittent; while remittent cases remain practically intermittent. This fact alone gives an enormous value to the treatment, for all who have had experience of the expectant plan must have noticed the startling rapidity with which heart-failure frequently supervenes in cases where a continuously-high temperature is allowed to remain unchecked.

But more than this is claimed for the treatment. Tripier and Bouveret, from a study of eighty-four charts, find that, if the mean of eight daily observations before the baths be taken, the average temperature of the first day of bathing, so arrived at, forms a maximum which is never afterwards exceeded; and that this is true no matter at what stage of the disease the treatment is commenced. They conclude, therefore, that defervescence commences from the first day of the treatment.

After treating a considerable number of my own charts in the same manner, I can confirm the statement that in the large majority the average temperature during the first day's treatment, estimated from numerous observations taken just before each bath, has been higher than that of any day that followed. Now Tripier and Bouveret seem to regard this as indicating an alteration in the tendency of the temperature, which in consequence of being frequently reduced steadily loses its power to rise. This may be so, but allowance must be made for the fact, that during the first day's treatment the baths are comparatively short—their duration is more or less experimental in fact—so that their antipyretic action could not be expected to be so great as during the following days, when the intensity of the fever has been accurately gauged.

Circulatory Symptoms

In pyrexia of any sort, with rare exceptions, the action of the heart is accelerated. In typhoid this acceleration is usually slight at first, but it undergoes a progressive increase, until in the advanced stages of the fever great rapidity may be attained. The acceleration is stated to be due in the first instance to the direct action of the warmer blood on the endocardium. It is probably also in part due to the relaxation of the cutaneous vessels, leading to a somewhat reduced general blood-pressure. Later on another factor is added in the pyrexial degeneration of the heart-tissue and the consequent enfeeblement of its muscular power. Weak and insufficient contractions are then compensated for to some extent by greater

41

rapidity. That the last is the explanation of the constantly-increasing rapidity of the pulse in the advanced stages of the fever there can be no doubt.

Along with the increased rapidity there always occur other signs of feebleness, in particular more or less impairment and shortening of the systolic sound, and smallness together with compressibility and sometimes irregularity of the pulse. These changes in the circulation are, generally speaking, marked in proportion to the duration and average height of the preceding pyrexia, and they are apt to supervene with great rapidity in those cases where the temperature has been both high and unremitting. They have always been rightly regarded as of grave prognostic significance, and it is therefore of the highest importance that they should be anticipated or retarded if possible.

The first effect of a cold bath is an acceleration of the pulse. This is probably due to nervousness, for it is most obvious in women and in patients of a timid disposition. After a time, varying in different individuals, a fall in the rate sets in, and this is as a rule continued after the bath is over, and down to the point of the greatest reduction in the temperature. During the stationary period of the temperature the pulse continues unchanged, and then rises with the temperature until they both regain their former height. In cases where shivering comes on towards the end of the bath, there may be a second acceleration in the pulse-rate, but this is temporary only and passes off with the former.

The *rationale* of the action of the bath in reducing the pulse-rate is probably complex. That the circulation of cooler blood in and through the organ itself is an important factor is probable, inasmuch as the pulse-rate and the temperature fall and rise for the most part simultaneously. Since, however, it happens at times that the pulse is lowered in frequency before the internal temperature of the body has been reduced, or even in spite of a rise, plainly some additional explanation is required. It is stated that the cutaneous vascular constriction which occurs on immersion is not fully compensated for by the collateral hyperæmia in the muscular layer, and that consequently a general rise of blood-pressure takes place. If this is so it would tend to cause slower and more vigorous action of the heart. It is not possible to establish any definite numerical proportion between the reduction in the temperature and that in the pulse-rate. At a given stage in any one case, it will be true that the greater the fall in temperature, the greater will be the retardation in the pulse-rate ; but this does not hold good for different stages of the same case, nor for different cases.

43

The chief condition which modifies the action of the bath on the pulse-rate is the stage of the disease. As a general rule the pulse-rate is more readily reduced at the beginning of the fever, the reverse having been shown to be the case with the temperature. Putting aside those cases where the pulse-rate is but very slightly raised above the normal, and where consequently no great reduction is to be expected, it is always an unfavourable sign when, after a successful heat-abstraction, the pulse-rate fails to be appreciably retarded; for in such cases there are usually other indications of failure of the circulation.

Coincident with the alteration in rate, the pulse undergoes a manifest alteration in character. Before the bath it was probably large and soft, possibly dicrotous; on immersion it becomes much smaller and harder, and dicrotism, if present, disappears, or at any rate becomes less noticeable. Unlike the fall in rate, the alteration in character comes on immediately, persists to some extent during the bath, and for some time afterwards, gradually disappearing as the temperature rises. It always attains its maximum intensity immediately after immersion, and usually remits somewhat during the continuance of the bath. It is due of course to the contraction of the artery, and is part of the cutaneous anæmia already alluded to. It is most marked in the early

44

stages of the disease, when it may be excessive, the pulse being reduced to a mere thread, and the extremities becoming pallid. Later on it is much less apparent. Thus the period of greatest cutaneous anæmia coincides with that during which the temperature is most difficult to reduce, and *vice versâ*. This is again confirmatory of the truth of Winternitz's theory as to the importance of the cutaneous circulation in the automatic heat-regulating function of the body. It is probable, therefore, that the easy reducibility of the temperature in the later stages of typhoid, which is usually attributed to circulatory feebleness, is more accurately explained by a certain impotence in the automatic heat-regulating mechanism, although doubtless the two causes are always operating at the same time.

The smallness of the radial pulse, due to arterial constriction, has frequently led to error. No less an authority than Dr Alexander Collie, in his Belfast address, states that " in severe cases the remedy [the bath] was inadmissible owing to its depressing effect, . . . but above all to its definite and marked effect upon the circulation, which it invariably greatly weakened." Contraction of the superficial arteries owing to cold is of course a physiological phenomenon, observable in healthy persons taking their morning tub; yet it would hardly occur to any one to say that in them the circulation is weakened. And, in conditions of fever, nothing is more certain than that a properly-applied cold bath is a tonic to the circulation. This fact alone will explain many of its beneficial results.

The ultimate effect of a systematic course of cold-bathing is pretty nearly what might have been anticipated from the above. It is undisputed that the progressive acceleration of the pulse, in the later stages of the fever, is an index of the degeneration of the cardiac muscle, and that this is in turn mainly caused by the persistence and severity of the pyrexia. Anything which mitigates the last might be expected, therefore, to prevent or at any rate moderate the former two. Still it is advisable that this anticipation should be clinically confirmed. Confirmation was sought for in the following manner. Two series of charts were selected, equal in number ; the one from the " expectant " year, 1886, the other from the first three years of the " bath-period." Every care was taken in the selection to render the two series comparable, the following points being especially attended to—the day of fever on admission ; general course, character, and duration of temperature ; the absence of complications of all kinds, and of symptoms due to the intestinal lesion. A comparison of the two series showed that the progressive acceleration in the pulse-rate was deferred and rendered less marked in the cases treated by cold-bathing. Again, another series of cases was taken from the " bath-period," similar in all respects, except that they were admitted at a later stage of the fever. In these it was found that the check on the acceleration of the pulse-rate, though present, was less noticeable.

What is true of the mere acceleration of the pulse, is true also of its other characters. As just mentioned, in all cases of any duration there is a tendency for the pulse to become smaller, more compressible, and less distinct, but in those treated by systematic cold-bathing, and more especially in those so treated from near the commencement, these changes are deferred in their onset, and do not reach the same degree of severity.

Hence the conclusion that the treatment prevented to a great extent the progressively-increasing feebleness of the circulation, but that its power in this respect was much impaired by delay in commencing it.

By far the most conclusive proof, however, of the beneficial action of the treatment on the circulation, will be found on considering the mortality. There it is evident that the complications and modes of death which are directly dependent on circulatory failure are precisely those which have been rendered less frequent during the " bath-period."

Respiratory Symptoms and Complications

The immediate effect of the bath on the respiratory movements of the typhoid patient resembles that which is observed in a healthy subject. There is always a disturbance of rhythm, but as to its usual character there is some difference of opinion. It has been described as a long inspiration, followed by a momentary closure of the glottis, and then by a long expiration; but respiration may be only impeded, or it may be short, gasping, and frequent. The effect probably varies widely, but in any case the immediate alteration in rhythm is purely nervous in origin, and is due to the action of cold on the sensory nerves of the skin. The signs of shock, however, last but a minute or two, and are succeeded by regular respirations which are always deepened. These may be accelerated, unaltered, or more commonly, according to my experience, slightly diminished in frequency; but all agree that they are decidedly deeper, and this from a therapeutic point of view is the most important result.

In most cases of typhoid some bronchial catarrh is present, although often not enough to cause any noticeable cough so long as the patient remains undisturbed in bed. But the powerful inspiratory movements which follow immersion lead to a sudden displacement of mucus; cough is thereby induced,

48

and the tubes are efficiently cleared. Not infrequently, then, the bath gives the first information
as to the existence of a bronchial catarrh.

Usually where cough is already present, it is
slight, irritative, and ineffectual; the effect of the
bath is then to increase and render it more powerful,
sometimes even to set up a paroxysm of coughing.
Very soon the benefit of the regular clearing of the
air-passages so induced is apparent; the patient,
who had previously been troubled by constant
respiratory irritation, coughs now a few times only
on first entering the bath, and later on even this
ceases.

In all cases the respiratory comfort which follows
the bath is apparent to the bystander in the increased freedom and extent of the chest-movements,
while the sense of weight and constriction is completely, although it may be at first only temporarily,
relieved. *In no case has a bronchitis been set up,
nor has one that was pre-existent been intensified.*

The fear of inducing pneumonia has probably had
more to do with postponing the general adoption of
the cold-bath treatment than any other of the
imaginary dangers attributed to it. As usual the
fear is the outcome of pure theory, and rests upon
no more solid basis than the popular terror of
catching cold. That the danger does not exist is
proved by the fact that *pneumonia is precisely one*

of the complications that is rendered infrequent by systematic bathing.

This could be demonstrated by comparing the percentage of its occurrences during the periods of expectancy and bathing respectively; but in the present instance there would remain a doubt as to the accuracy of such a comparison, since it is probable that some of the slighter cases were left unrecorded in the former series. More precise, and in view of the high mortality of the complication in question, equally conclusive evidence can be adduced by comparing the number of cases in which it led to a fatal result in either period (see Chap. V). To understand the beneficial influence of the treatment in averting pneumonia it is essential to distinguish clearly between the different forms of the disease. Three varieties are commonly described—(1) Croupous or lobar pneumonia; (2) Catarrhal, lobular, or broncho-pneumonia; and (3) Hypostatic pneumonia. The last is more properly termed hypostatic engorgement, since inflammatory processes enter but slightly into its pathology. Its cause is gradual failure of the circulatory and respiratory functions, whereby gravitation is permitted to exercise a preponderating influence on the pulmonary circulation. While therefore it no doubt contributes to the fatal issue, it is to be regarded rather as a concomitant, frequent but incidental, than as a substantive cause of death. Accordingly, in the mortality list, it is excluded from the causes of death in connexion with the respiratory system, and is referred to "exhaustion."

Croupous and broncho-pneumonia are, on the contrary, definite causes of death. The latter is admittedly by far the most common, and as to its pathology there is but little difference of opinion. Just as when it occurs in other affections, it is consequent on bronchitis, and is immediately due either to simple extension of the inflammatory process into the air-vesicles, or more probably in the main to alveolar collapse. In typhoid, conditions that are especially favourable for its development usually exist: more or less marked circulatory failure, leading to capillary engorgement and stasis; mental torpor, preventing a due appreciation of the necessity for coughing; and muscular enfeeblement, causing shallow respiratory movements, imperfect pulmonary inflation, and inefficient coughing efforts. When in addition there is appreciable tympanitic distension of the abdomen, which not only by interfering with the descent of the diaphragm prevents the expansion of the lower portions of the lung, but also by mechanically pressing on the heart seriously damages its power, it is evident that almost every condition favourable for the development of broncho-pneumonia is presented at one and the same time.

Hence it is that this complication most frequently supervenes gradually, and at an advanced stage of the fever.

Now cold-bathing markedly and most happily influences each and all of the above-mentioned conditions. Its effect in causing full pulmonary expansion and the expulsion of mucus-plugs from the bronchi has been already referred to. It maintains the sensorium in a state of remarkable lucidity; it is an efficient prophylactic against muscular and circulatory failure; and it has an undoubted power to prevent and abolish flatulent distension of the hollow abdominal viscera. Thus its efficiency against the bronchial form of pneumonia is easy to understand.

With regard to croupous pneumonia the case is different. This variety does not supervene gradually in the later stages of the fever; its onset is usually sudden, and it may occur at any period of the disease, even at its commencement. Neither is it necessarily preceded by bronchial catarrh or by marked circulatory failure, although it may lead to the latter with great rapidity.

As to what constitutes its pathology, we must remain for the present uncertain. Possibly it may turn out to be a secondary infection, by the pneumococcus or other microbe, superadded to the original specific infection of the fever;

and many considerations seem to point in that direction.

At any rate its ætiology differs widely from that of the bronchial form, and consequently we could hardly anticipate for the bath-treatment an equally efficient prophylactic action against it. This is borne out by an analysis of the six cases of fatal chest-affections that occurred during the "bath-period."

Nervous and Psychical Symptoms

By far the most conspicuous effect of the cold-bath treatment is that which it exerts upon the symptoms in connexion with the nervous system. Just as in health, the first shock of immersion is immediately followed by some gasping respirations and a certain degree of *shivering*. This shivering is always to some extent under control, and in most cases passes off in a minute or two. It must not be confounded with what has been called the "true shivering" that comes on towards the end of the bath, which indicates the beginning of the fall of temperature of the interior of the body. The latter is more violent, and instead of gradually abating, steadily increases in severity if the bath be prolonged. Generally it subsides shortly after the patient has been replaced in bed, but in some cases it persists for half-an-hour or even longer. In some

53

very nervous subjects the initial shiver is continued throughout the bath, and gradually merges into the other; but it rarely happens that there is not a short interval during which the patient is free from this rather unpleasant symptom. "True shivering" is almost always present when immersion has been sufficiently prolonged, and in some plans of bathing it forms the signal for the termination of the bath.

Headache during the early stages of the fever is an almost constant symptom. It usually disappears during or immediately after the first bath, but recurs as the temperature re-ascends. In many cases, however, it ceases permanently after a day or two of regular treatment; and with it disappear other related symptoms, such as flushing of the face, throbbing of the temples, etc.

Insomnia in cases treated systematically is almost unknown. Shortly after each bath, when shivering has ceased, the patient experiences a sensation of great comfort and well-being. This is soon followed by drowsiness and deep refreshing sleep. The depth of this sleep gradually decreases as the temperature rises, but as a rule patients have to be waked for their baths. Although in this way their rest is frequently broken, yet the total amount of sleep obtained is in excess of that under simple expectancy, and there can be little doubt that it is of better quality. One case only have I known in which bathing had an exactly opposite effect. In the patient in question, dread of the bath was so extreme that it actually prevented sleep altogether, and consequently the bathing had to be discontinued.

In almost all cases *restlessness* is abolished, and the expression of the face is bright, cheerful, and natural, contrasting strongly with the listless indifference of the ordinary typhoid patient. This is consequent on the great mitigation of the sensation of *malaise*.

Delirium and *stupor* are rare symptoms. They hardly ever arise during the course of the treatment, and when present on admission they generally subside quickly. It is not uncommon to see the milder forms disappear after one bath, but severe cases may require two or three days of bathing. Cases where these symptoms persist in spite of the treatment are quite uncommon, and there is often in them some cause, in addition to the fever, to account for the mental state, such as excessive alcoholism, hereditary taint of insanity, etc. Still more rare is it for either symptom to arise during the continuance of the bathing. But the power of the treatment to maintain the sensorium in a lucid state is strongly demonstrated by the fact, that it is not uncommon for delirium to arise for the first time when the baths are stopped. This holds good

55

whatever be the circumstances necessitating the suspension ; whether it be the onset of some contra-indicating complication such as hæmorrhage or perforation, or simply a falling temperature which indicates the approach of convalescence.

During the two years 1888 and 1889, 934 cases of typhoid were admitted, and out of these delirium or stupor occurred in 71, or 7·60 per cent. Murchison found these symptoms present in 67 per cent. of all his cases, and Pepper (1893) says, " delirium of some sort may be observed at times in the majority of cases."

Even more convincing, however, is a consideration of the circumstances under which the symptoms arose in these seventy-one cases. All the nine cases of stupor, and twenty-five of those of delirium, presented the symptom on admission. Of the remaining thirty-seven, twenty-four became delirious for the first time only after the cessation of the baths; and two cases were not bathed at all. There remain only eleven, therefore, out of the 934 admitted, in which any kind of mental disturbance arose during the continuance of the bathing, and in which consequently the symptom could be said to have arisen in spite of it.

The assertion that the occurrence of mental symptoms has been reduced by the bath-treatment from over 50 per cent. to less than eight, will appear to many as the unconscious exaggeration of an enthusiast; but on looking back I am confident that it is within the truth. The change in the aspect of the Fever-wards, after the introduction of the treatment, was so great that it was apparent to even the most inexperienced employee.

Under the old treatment it had been a rule, and a very necessary one, that the ward-doors should be kept constantly locked to prevent the sudden escape of a delirious patient; but afterwards doors as well as windows were allowed to remain widely open night and day. It is to be remembered that, owing to the manner in which the treatment was introduced, the change in the condition of the wards was not gradual, but sudden and complete, and therefore patent to all.

As might be expected, all other symptoms indicating *nervous and muscular prostration* are rendered much less common. Involuntary evacuations, tremors, spasmodic movements such as subsultus, carphology, etc., occur only in rare instances, and then almost always in cases where some accident or complication has necessitated the cessation of the treatment, or in patients admitted in the last stages of the disease.

The *rationale* of the action of the bath in preventing and relieving nervous symptoms is probably complex. That these symptoms are in great part dependent on the temperature is evident from the facts—(1) that they are as a rule in proportion to the height of the temperature, increasing and decreasing as the latter rises and falls, and (2) that they can be ameliorated or abolished by measures that reduce the temperature, such as antipyretic drugs. But there can be no doubt that the external application of cold possesses an influence over nervous symptoms, independently of its action on the temperature. For delirium or stupor may pass off very rapidly in the first bath, before there has been time for the temperature to be appreciably lowered, or even when the thermometer has shown it to be actually raised.

Schüller has shown that a cold bath causes an immediate expansion of the vessels of the pia-mater, which lasts during the immersion, and afterwards makes way for a contraction or a varying condition. Inversely a warm full-bath almost always produces a powerful contraction of the pia-mater vessels, which is followed by a short expansion, either during the bathing, if this is protracted, or after it is over. He considers the contraction of the pia-mater vessels in a warm bath, and their expansion in a cold bath, to be secondary or collateral actions of the alteration in the calibre of the cutaneous vessels induced by the bath.

The immediate action of the cold bath is thus

a strong and prompt stimulant to the brain and nervous system. This is certainly its most conspicuous effect, and recently some authorities have gone so far as to assert that this is the only action that is worthy of consideration. Consequently they have reserved the cold bath for cases showing symptoms of somnolence, stupor, etc., allowing these states to arise before resorting to its use. This is decidedly a retrograde movement, and is entirely inconsistent with an intelligent conception of the prophylactic value of the treatment; for surely it is irrational to rest content with the chance of successfully combating symptoms when these can almost to a certainty be prevented.

Digestive Symptoms

The effect of the bath-treatment on the digestive disturbances associated with typhoid will best be demonstrated by a detailed consideration of the various portions of the alimentary canal.

A very marked influence is exerted on the condition of the tongue and mouth, and on the secretion of *saliva*. Although under expectancy many, even fatal, cases pass through all the stages of typhoid without the tongue ever being at any time dry and brown, yet the majority if at all severe do exhibit this symptom associated with *sordes* on the lips and teeth. In these cases the salivary and other secretions of the buccal cavity are often in complete abeyance.

In cases treated by systematic cold-bathing from an early stage of the fever, or even before the tongue has become dry and brown, these symptoms certainly arise only in a small minority. In many cases where treatment is not commenced until after their appearance, they are completely dispelled after a day or two; while in the remainder, if not actually dispelled, they are very greatly mitigated.

The immediate effect of each individual bath is most striking. Before it, the tongue may have been red and dry at the tip and edges, and coated brown and dry down the centre. Shortly after immersion the tip and edges become moist, and later on the central strip changes to a thick moist white coating. The tongue retains this appearance for a time after the bath; usually with the return of pyrexia it reverts to its previous condition, though not as a rule to the same extent. In the milder cases the dryness is abolished permanently after a few baths; in others it is but checked and prevented from increasing. The old well-known dry, shrivelled, almost black tongue is never in my experience met with, except in an odd case brought into hospital in the typhoid state.

What has been said of the dry brown tongue, applies in an even greater degree to sordes, which, except in a very mild form, and in a few cases, have become practically unknown since the introduction of the bath-treatment. The mode in which the treatment was introduced threw into bold relief the improvement in symptoms which followed; and in no class of symptoms except the nervous was the improvement more conspicuous than in those relating to the mouth and tongue.

Before the treatment had been introduced many weeks, it was a common subject for remark among the nursing staff, that the difficulty always before experienced in keeping the mouths of the patients clean had practically ceased to exist. While previously it had taken hours to effect the toilette of the mouth and teeth, it had now become unnecessary to do anything except see that the patients used an antiseptic mouth-wash occasionally. One great source of annoyance was almost entirely done away with. In Brisbane, at most seasons of the year, flies are extremely troublesome. They settled in swarms on patients with sordes who were in the typhoid state, and who usually slept with their mouths open, so that frequently the lips, teeth, and tongue were coated with black masses of flies. It was impossible except in a slight degree to mitigate the nuisance. After the bath-treatment was introduced all this was changed; sordes were rare; patients usually breathed naturally through the nose; and the fly-nuisance became a thing of the past. This observation was made in the first instance by the nursing staff.

From the improvement in the state of the buccal cavity, it naturally follows that *thirst* is greatly lessened and appetite improved. Thirst indeed in many cases is never complained of at all, patients being quite satisfied with their allowance of milk, and not asking for other liquid in addition.

Appetite (*i. e.* for solids) does not, except in rare cases, re-appear during the severity of the fever, no matter how thoroughly this may be controlled by the bathing. Yet under the bath-treatment it does frequently re-appear with the first indications of approaching convalescence, even before the discontinuance of the bathing, *i. e.* at a much earlier stage than is observed under expectant methods.

Owing to the comparatively healthy condition of the saliva, the sense of *taste* is rarely lost, patients expressing preferences for different kinds of liquid diet, instead of as previously exhibiting absolute indifference on the point.

The symptoms just considered undoubtedly owe their existence in the main to the elevation of the temperature—for (1) they can be produced artificially in animals by simply raising the temperature; (2) they are more or less common to all pyrexial diseases; and (3) their severity as a rule is in proportion to the height of the temperature. But in all cases a certain duration of the temperature is required for their production, and consequently they appear only in exceptional instances during the earliest stages.

The power of the bath to avert or abolish them lies chiefly in its antipyretic effect; yet from the experience of some cases it would appear that it has in addition a more direct and independent action, similar to what it undoubtedly has upon the nervous symptoms. Very many cases go through a long attack of fever without any dryness of the mouth and tongue, until, in accordance with Brand's rule, the necessity for bathing has ceased. They then develop for the first time dryness and even brownness of the tongue, though never to a severe extent. In these circumstances the patient often demands that the bathing be recommenced, and a short occasional bath is always found to dispel the symptom. Since, therefore, these symptoms arise under a lower average temperature in the absence of the bathing, it would seem necessary to assume that the bath has some special power over them, other than that which it possesses in virtue of its antipyretic action.

Just as in the case of the saliva, there can be little doubt that cold-bathing tends to re-establish the secretion of *gastric juice*, which is more or less in abeyance in all fevers. At any rate, it is certain that gastric symptoms are much less common.

Vomiting is stated by Murchison to have been present in about 36 per cent. of his cases. I am not able to give the exact percentage of its occurrence under the bath-treatment, but I am certain it was under 15 per cent.; and even in these it was almost always due to some definite exciting cause, such as a dose of quinine, or was simply a symptom of general peritonitis. The absence of the extreme anorexia, usually noted, points to a state of the gastric secretion more nearly approaching the normal.

It is probable that the secretions of the *pancreas* and *intestinal glands* are all somewhat improved by cold-bathing, since digestion undoubtedly is. It has frequently been remarked after a few days' treatment, that undigested curds cease to be passed.

Diarrhœa and Meteorism

Hostile critics have constantly stated that the bath-treatment must seriously increase the severity of the abdominal symptoms, and especially the *diarrhœa*. That the opposite is the case it will not be difficult to show.

Murchison states that diarrhœa is the rule in typhoid; he noted it in 93 out of 100 cases.

Other observers have come to a different conclusion; Collie puts it at a much lower figure, in fact he regards it as exceptional. At the Brisbane Hospital, during the first six months of 1886 ("expectant period"), out of 351 consecutive cases, 181 are noted as suffering from diarrhœa, or 52 per cent. During the years 1888 and 1889 ("bath period"), out of 934 cases admitted, 363 had diarrhœa or loose motions, a percentage of 39.

The real difference in favour of the bath-treatment is greater, for, during the former period, hardly more than the cases where the severity of the diarrhœa was sufficient to demand treatment were noted; whereas, during the latter, notes as to the state of the bowels were kept in every instance, cases which had only two or three loose motions *per diem* being included.

Cases in which the treatment is commenced before the onset of diarrhœa but rarely develop this symptom in a severe form. When, however, it is present on admission, the first effects of the cold bath would appear at a superficial glance to support the contention that the symptom is increased. Here the patient will probably have an evacuation immediately after each bath, so that the number of motions in the twenty-four hours is increased. This is but temporary, however; in the course of a day or two the patient has a motion only after the bath, those in the interval having ceased; and later on those following the baths only occur occasionally.

Co-existing with the diarrhœa, there is usually some degree of *meteorism*. In these cases cold-bathing is quickly followed by the passage of large quantities of flatus with the motions. Soon the abdomen, which may have been more or less distended and tympanitic, becomes flaccid and retracted. In the cases where bathing only is resorted to, the distension recurs to some extent by the end of the three-hours interval, to be again dispelled by the succeeding bath. The application of a large abdominal ice-bag, however, kept constantly filled during the interval between the baths, almost invariably prevents the recurrence of the meteorism; it not only prolongs the effect of the bath in this direction but intensifies it, so that the flaccidity and retraction of the abdomen progressively increase. At the same time the stools, which have now been rendered less frequent, undergo a well-marked alteration in character. Their consistence increases, they become more uniform, and the passage of undigested curd diminishes or ceases altogether. Thenceforward, two or three moderately loose motions *per diem* is the rule, an amount of evacuation that is probably beneficial: in some cases indeed actual constipation supervenes.

In certain cases meteorism may be present without diarrhœa, or even in association with constipation; in these it is the rule for large quantities of flatus to be passed in each bath.

As in other instances, the grounds for the contention that the treatment would increase diarrhœa are purely theoretical. It is said that the application of cold externally, by contracting the capillary areas of the skin, must induce a corresponding vascular dilatation of internal organs, amongst them of the intestinal mucosa, and so give rise to congestion. The objection would appear to be based upon a faulty estimate of the relative importance of the factors concerned in the ætiology of diarrhœa.

To begin with, it is improbable that congestion or catarrh plays any important part in the causation of diarrhœa in typhoid. Cohnheim has shown that catarrhal inflammation of the mucous membrane between the ulcers is quite uncommon; and in the Post-mortem room at the Brisbane Hospital hyperæmia was almost invariably found to be limited to a narrow zone immediately surrounding the ulcers. Cohnheim further points out that the assumption of intestinal catarrh is quite unnecessary, for the diarrhœa is essentially the result of deficient absorption of the watery portion of the intestinal contents; consequently anything which interferes with absorption may cause it to arise. Absorption takes place in proportion to the length of time the contents of the intestine remain in contact with the absorbents, and therefore anything which considerably reduces this time will infallibly set up diarrhœa. Hence it is that exaggerated peristaltic action, however induced, is by far the most important and the commonest factor in its causation.

In the diarrhœa of typhoid the causative factors are probably operative in the following order—(1) ulceration exposing the nerve-endings and irritation conveyed therefrom to the myenteric plexus; (2) increased peristalsis; (3) increased rapidity of the intestinal current; and (4) consequent defective absorption of watery matter, which is passed *per anum*. That this is the true pathology of typhoid diarrhœa is rendered the more probable—(1) by the resemblance which the stools bear to the contents of the small intestine; (2) by the fact that the onset of diarrhœa is usually coincident in point of time with the commencement of the separation of the sloughs, *i. e.* with the formation of ulcers (were congestion sufficient to explain the diarrhœa, there seems no reason why it should not occur considerably sooner, even from the first during the process of glandular infiltration, or why it should be absent in abortive cases); (3) by the fact that the severity of the diarrhœa is in proportion, generally speaking, to the extent of mucous surface ulcerated, but more particularly to the extent so affected in the large intestine. This last fact was placed beyond a doubt by the practice in the Brisbane Hospital of holding post-mortem examinations systematically in all cases. In those cases especially where the so-called serous diarrhœa had been at all severe, the cæcum always, and not infrequently nearly the whole length of the colon, were found to be extensively diseased. That this should be so is no matter for surprise, for it is of course mainly in the large intestine that the absorption of water takes place, and therefore rapidity of passage through this portion of the alimentary canal, more than any other, tends to diminish the consistence of the fæces.

Meteorism, which is due to a paresis of the intestine, and is therefore one result of the over-stimulation of the musculature, becomes, when developed, an additional factor in the causation of diarrhœa. Gaseous accumulation, by distending the gut, compresses and stretches the blood-vessels, thus lessening their calibre and diminishing their absorptive power.

Cold abdominal applications would seem in the first instance to cause an increase in the peristaltic movements of the intestine. Later on, however, there succeeds a slowing of the movements, approaching a state of aperistalsis, accompanied by increased tone of the muscular fibre. This is necessarily followed by a retardation of the alimentary current, and a more rapid absorption of liquid, while it effectually prevents a re-accumulation of flatus.

The action of external cold thus essentially differs from that of opiates. Opium certainly checks diarrhœa, and there seems to be no doubt that it does so by diminishing peristalsis. Its action, however, is so frequently followed by the appearance of abdominal distension as to lead to the conclusion that the diminished peristalsis so induced tends to pass into a state of intestinal paresis.

It is thus apparent that most of the important factors associated with the causation of typhoid diarrhœa are favourably modified by cold-water treatment, and it is difficult therefore to conceive of a remedy, short of one that would act directly on the intestinal ulceration, that is more completely adapted to the condition of a typhoid patient, presenting the usual indications of severe abdominal disease.

Perforation and Hæmorrhage

No question of course arises as to the influence of the treatment on these complications when they have already occurred, since both perforation and hæmorrhage constitute absolute contra-indications to further bathing, at any rate for the time being. But it is important to determine what influence, if any, is exerted upon their frequency by the treatment. On this point diametrically opposite opinions are expressed. The opponents of cold-bathing point out that, especially in the later stages of the fever, the floors of the ulcers are often extremely thin, consisting at times of peritoneum only; and on this account it is contended that the moving of the patient necessary for bathing is fraught with imminent danger of causing rupture. Hæmorrhage they aver must be rendered more frequent by reason of the congestion of internal organs following upon the cutaneous anæmia induced by the bath. Even at the Middlesex Hospital, where the bath was at one time, under Cayley, used boldly and systematically, timidity on the score of intestinal accidents has recently led to its discontinuance in the later stages of the disease.

Brand, on the other hand, states that if the treatment is commenced at the very beginning of the fever, and is carried out consistently thenceforward, perforation and hæmorrhage, in common with all other complications, are prevented. He is careful to say, however, that it is only when the treatment is commenced before the fourth day of the fever that this holds good, and herein he draws a sharp line of demarcation between these two intestinal accidents and the other common complications of the disease. For whereas the latter, such as pneu-

71

monia, etc., are rendered infrequent in proportion as the treatment is commenced early, the power of averting the former complications is altogether lost after the fourth day.

He concludes, therefore, that when commenced before the fourth day, and carried through systematically, the treatment exerts a modifying influence upon the ulcerative process, and he adduces the following argument in support of his view : " In the case of a typhoid patient treated from the beginning, and strictly according to the rule, symptoms in connexion with the alimentary canal disappear almost completely ; the mouth is moist ; the tongue clean ; thirst is relieved ; the appetite re-appears ; there is no meteorism, diarrhœa, or gurgling in the iliac fossa ; and the motions are natural. In these circumstances it is hard to conceive that there is a serious ulcerative lesion in the intestine." [1]

It is to be remarked, in the first place, that the arguments of the opponents of cold-bathing are purely theoretical, no facts having been adduced in their support. Even without the aid of facts, however, it will not, I think, be difficult to show that the theories are fallacious.

The only form of hæmorrhage in typhoid which is of the slightest consequence is due not to conges-

---

[1] *La fièvre typhoïde traitée par les bains froids*, by MM. R. Tripier and L. Bouveret. Paris 1886.

tion but to ulceration, involving and laying open a vessel of some size. Nor has it ever been proved that cold-bathing causes congestion of the mucous surface of the bowel; there is indeed good reason for believing that the opposite condition is induced; and certainly the application of an ice-bag to the abdomen is a time-honoured therapeutic measure for this complication.

The frequency of intestinal hæmorrhage is stated by Louis to be 6 per cent.; Murchison found it in 58 out of 1564 cases, or in 3·7 per cent., but his figures relate only to copious hæmorrhage—over six ounces. At the Brisbane Hospital during the first three years of the "bath period," out of 1173 cases 85 had hæmorrhage, a percentage of 7·2; but among these are included all cases, even where the blood lost was a mere trace. Unfortunately I am not able to institute a comparison in this respect with the "expectant period" at Brisbane, since during that time record was kept only of the severer cases. Liebermeister, however, found a slight decrease in the frequency of intestinal hæmorrhage under cold-bathing; of 861 cases expectantly treated 8·4 per cent. had hæmorrhage; of 882 bathed, 6·2 per cent. Further evidence as to the absence of increased danger from bleeding is to be found by comparing the frequency of fatal hæmorrhage in the two periods (see Chap. V).

The danger of inducing perforation has, I am inclined to think, been much over-rated. In the first place, though it may seem that to lift an adult patient out of bed and lower him into a bath must entail considerable exertion on his part, yet this is not necessarily true. The danger to the weakened intestine must be measured by the force with which the abdominal muscles contract, and if the lifting be conducted with ordinary skill, and as above described by means of the stretcher, this is reduced to a minimum. Certainly no more forcible contraction need occur than when a patient is moved upon his side in an ordinary changing, or than during defæcation ; and this, be it noted, is especially true of the later stages of the fever, for by that time the patient has in most cases long since been educated to minimise muscular effort during the manœuvre.

That perforation often follows some exertion, usually straining at stool, is undeniable ; but I believe that in most of these instances, the ulcer would in all probability have given way in any case, and that the muscular effort simply precipitated the accident. In support of this is the fact, that it is very rare at necropsies to find anything resembling a rent in the bowel. In forty post-mortem examinations of cases in which perforation had taken place, this condition was found in one only, and here there was an ordinary perforation in addition.

74

The great majority of perforations are large or small, according as they have occurred at the time of slough-separation or later. In the first variety they are due to the primary depth of the necrotic process, involving the whole or nearly the whole thickness of the intestinal wall. The necrosis of the peritoneum may be primary, or may follow the loss of its blood-supply through death of the subjacent muscular coat. In the second variety of perforation, there is a failure of cicatrisation. This is replaced by a continuous burrowing process of ulceration, which finally reaches and destroys the peritoneum. In either case muscular action may, and probably always does, determine the actual occurrence of perforation. But it is to be observed that what really takes place is not a forcible rending of a thinned membrane, but rather the displacement of a loosened patch of necrotic tissue. Manifestly, to effect this so little force is necessary, that the danger must be imminent at every movement of the patient and even at every peristalsis of the intestine. Probably, therefore, it is only in those cases where the muscular action which precedes perforation is one of which we have distinct cognisance, such as straining at stool, vomiting, sitting up in bed, etc., that we refer the accident to its proper immediate cause.

But whether these considerations be accepted or

not, there is plenty of direct evidence to show that the danger of inducing perforation by cold-bathing is practically *nil*. During the first three years of the "bath period," upwards of 25,000 baths were administered ; during this time thirty-five cases suffered perforation, but in two only did the accident happen in, or immediately after, a bath. Considering that many of the patients were in the aggregate several days in the water, this is certainly not more than might have been expected, on the assumption of a purely fortuitous relation between the treatment and the accident. But even if the responsibility of the bathing in the above two cases could be fully substantiated, the potent influence of the treatment in moderating meteorism and other intestinal symptoms would be more than sufficient compensation. Since the occurrence and the mortality of perforation are practically identical, the most conclusive evidence of the harmlessness of the treatment in this respect will be found in considering the death-rate.

Brand's *dictum* as to the power of the treatment to prevent perforation and hæmorrhage, when commenced before the fourth day, I cannot either confirm or refute. Only one case admitted before the fourth day died from any cause, and that was from profuse diarrhœa; but such cases were only fifty-seven in number, out of the 1173 cases classed as typhoid,

76

during the first three years of the "bath period." Three cases however, admitted on, and treated systematically from, the fourth day, died from these accidents, namely, from perforation, two, and from hæmorrhage, one ; and it is difficult to conceive that twenty-four hours' earlier treatment would have made the essential difference.

It seems probable that there is a fallacy underlying this conclusion of Brand's. Jürgensen was the first to point out that an essential feature of *typhus levissimus* (febricula, simple continued fever, and abortive typhoid) was its sudden commencement with high fever and great *malaise*. These cases invariably recover, the glandular intestinal deposit, if existent, probably undergoing resolution without ulceration, and therefore without endangering the integrity of the bowel. Plainly such cases would be most likely to apply for early admission ; and this has certainly been so at the Brisbane Hospital.

The classification into typhoid and febricula is seen to depend mainly on the duration of the pyrexia, all cases that convalesced earlier than the tenth day being referred to the latter. On examination it is found that while only the fifty-seven just mentioned of the 1173 cases in the typhoid list were admitted before the fourth day, the number of cases in the febricula list during the same period, who came in before this day, was 63 out of 201 at the lowest computation, and probably more.[1] The 201 cases referred to are not of course included in the statistics, but just the same tendency for the shorter cases to seek earlier admission is observable in the 1173 cases classed as typhoid. Here the fifty-seven admitted before the fourth day contained a much higher proportion of mild and abortive cases, *i. e.* cases which convalesced between the tenth and twenty-first days, than the remainder that were admitted later; their average duration being 17·4 days against 23·3 days, the average duration of the whole series. The difference is remarkable, and probably sufficient to account for the asserted power of the bath-treatment to prevent the two intestinal accidents, when applied from the beginning.

There is, of course, one alternative. It might be contended that the treatment, when commenced so early in the case, *caused* the fever to abort; but this is inconsistent with what we know of its mode of action, and no such virtue, so far as I am aware, has even been claimed for it since the time of Currie.

That the treatment when commenced at a stage

---

[1] Many of the cases of febricula convalesced shortly after admission before the history was taken. The previous duration of the fever was therefore sometimes not recorded.

later than the fourth day is impotent to avert the occurrence of either accident, does not require demonstration, since it is admitted on the other side.

Urinary Symptoms

Symptoms in connexion with the *bladder*, such as true retention and incontinence of urine, are met with almost solely in cases where mental disturbance is present. This being rare under cold-bathing, it follows that the symptoms under consideration are rendered less common. There is, however, a spurious form of retention which is common in hospital-practice under any treatment, namely, the retention which occurs on first admission, and which simply arises from the patient's inability to pass water while lying down, or through nervousness due to the presence of others.

The modifications in the urinary secretion which ensue under the bath-treatment are fully dealt with in the work of MM. Tripier and Bouveret. During the course of the fever under expectant treatment, the urine undergoes certain changes which are generally admitted by most authorities. During the time that the temperature is rising, and throughout the time when it remains more or less stationary, the quantity of urine gradually diminishes. It is at the same time high-coloured, acid,

79

and of high specific gravity (1020—1030); and all these characters are marked in proportion to the intensity of the fever. Towards the approach of convalescence the urine increases greatly in quantity, becomes pale, of low specific gravity, and neutral or even alkaline in reaction. This MM. Tripier and Bouveret term the "critical polyuria."

The effect of systematic cold-bathing is, according to these authors, to hasten the appearance of this critical polyuria; so that the urine often becomes clear, abundant, and of low specific gravity at a stage when, under ordinary treatment, it would still present all the characters of febrile urine. This they regard as one of the most, if not the most, remarkable effect of Brand's treatment.

My own observations are generally confirmatory, but I have to confess that they have not been sufficiently numerous nor conducted with sufficient accuracy to make them of much value. In attributing the early appearance of copious urine of low specific gravity to the action of the bath-treatment, it is to be remembered that Murchison frequently observed these characters before the cessation of the fever, and that the quantity may be expected to increase after the end of the second week in any circumstances.

However, there is no doubt that in every form

of the fever, systematic cold-bathing, if commenced early, increases the quantity of urine passed and reduces its specific gravity; and this, be it remembered, in spite of the fact that patients so treated, owing to the great diminution of thirst, take considerably less liquid. The change in the urine may occur in the absence of any permanent reduction in the temperature-range, but the marked polyuria referred to by MM. Tripier and Bouveret was not frequently observed in Brisbane, except where the temperature was on the down grade, and where this indicated the approach of convalescence.

Brand attributes the increased flow of urine which follows cold-bathing to the reduction in the febrile temperature; Winternitz regards it as due to the heightening of the pressure in the vascular system, induced by the shock of cold immersion; Tripier and Bouveret assume the existence of a reflex action between the sensory nerves of the skin and the vasomotor fibres of the kidney. But whichever hypothesis is adopted, it must not be forgotten that the action of the bath-treatment in checking sweating, and thereby throwing on the kidneys the necessity for increased excretion of water, is a subsidiary though not an unimportant factor.

As to the quantity of *urea* excreted in typhoid there is some difference of opinion. Most authorities assert that it is raised above the normal, in accordance with the increased febrile consumption of the body. In the few cases where I have carefully watched the effect of the treatment on the urine, the average daily excretion of solids was observed to fall somewhat after a few days' bathing; but the observations were insufficient to be conclusive. The influence of the treatment upon the production and elimination of urea (and of carbonic acid) is referred to below in discussing nutrition.

Albumin during the course of the fever may appear in the urine in one of two forms—(1) as a slight albuminous cloud, without casts or other indication of renal disease; (2) in considerable amount, sometimes associated with smoky appearance of the urine, and even with casts. The latter is of a grave significance, since it indicates nephritis, which is quite likely to lead to fatal uræmia. It certainly has not been rendered more frequent by cold-bathing, and although I am not prepared to demonstrate the opposite, yet from the action of the treatment in maintaining the renal secretion in a state approximating to the normal, it is fair to infer that the tendency to albuminuria is probably diminished.

The first variety of albuminuria is of common occurrence. It does not tend to run into the other form, nor is it of any serious import. It has been claimed that in the majority of cases, systematic

82

bathing causes it to clear up in the course of a few days. In Brisbane it was found to do so in some cases, but in the rest no influence was apparent.

In this connexion the experiments of Roque and Weil are of much importance. These observers claim to have shown that "in typhoid fever left to itself the toxic products manufactured by the bacillus and the organism itself are eliminated in part during the illness. The urotoxic co-efficient is double the normal; but this elimination is incomplete and is only completed during convalescence, for the hypertoxicity continues for four or five weeks after the cessation of the fever. In typhoid fever treated by cold baths the elimination of toxic products is enormous during the illness. The urotoxic co-efficient is five or six times the normal. The hypertoxicity diminishes as the general symptoms mend and as the temperature falls, so that when the period of apyrexia sets in the elimination of toxins has ceased."

Nutrition

From what has preceded it might almost be inferred that the tissues of the body undergo less degeneration under the bath-treatment than under any form of expectancy. Muscular strength is maintained in a remarkable manner, as is evidenced by the comparative rarity of the dorsal decubitus;

most patients, even throughout severe attacks, lie on the side quite as frequently as on the back, turning from one to the other from time to time without assistance. In a case published by me (*Australasian Medical Gazette*, December 1887), the patient, after undergoing an attack of great severity, during which the temperature before bathing varied for six days between 104° and 106°, and which lasted twenty-three days and required in all one hundred and eight baths, was able on the fifth day of convalescence, *i. e.* on the first day that he was allowed out of bed, to stand upright without assistance. This is no exceptional case.

The progressive *emaciation*, that occurs more or less in every case of typhoid, is greatly retarded by the bath-treatment. To those who have seen a number of cases treated in both ways, this requires no proof; it is self-evident. Nevertheless, it has been made the subject of special study by many, all of whom have arrived at practically the same conclusions.

The loss of weight suffered by the typhoid patient follows a fairly regular course. It is slight during the first few days, gradually increases during the continuance of the fever, and reaches its maximum in the third week (this of course applies only to typical cases). The weight remains stationary or nearly so for a time, and then increases more or less rapidly during convalescence. The increase, however, is as a rule less rapid than the decrease that took place during the fever.

MM. Tripier and Bouveret, from their own observations and those of Vogl and others, demonstrate conclusively that under the treatment by cold baths—(1) the loss of weight is actually less; and (2) the increase of weight during convalescence is more rapid than the decrease during the fever.

It is undisputed that the emaciation is in the main due to the rapid combustion that takes place in the tissues in association with high temperature. In the case of the muscular tissues, the diminution in volume is accompanied by distinct histological changes, namely, the well-known granular and albuminoid degenerations, common in varying degrees to all pyrexial diseases. Thus the check on the progressive emaciation exerted by systematic bathing is chiefly due to the reduction so induced in the average temperature. In proof of this it has been shown that the amount of both carbonic acid and urea eliminated is diminished by cold-bathing. According to Schroeder, the elimination of carbonic acid is influenced in almost exactly the same manner, and to the same degree, as the temperature, being at its minimum about half-an-hour after the bath, at the time when the temperature is lowest, and gradually increasing as the latter rises.

85

The diminution in the excretion of urea cannot be explained by its retention in the system, since the action of cold-bathing is undoubtedly diuretic. It follows therefore that there is a diminished production.

Nevertheless the whole question is no simple one. One of the first effects of cold-immersion is certainly a reflex increase in the production of heat, accompanied of course by an increased excretion of carbonic acid and an increased assumption of oxygen. Winternitz, however, has shown that "the magnitude of the reflex heat-production brought about by heat-abstraction does not depend upon the absolute amount of heat abstracted, but upon the amount of thermal nervous stimulation combined therewith. This reflexly-excited increase of heat-production takes place predominantly in the muscular layer, and is contemporaneous with the increase in the blood-supply and the actual elevation of the temperature caused therein by the cutaneous anæmia immediately succeeding immersion." "Cold increases the excretion of carbonic acid and nitrogen only so long as the temperature of the body and tissues is not reduced. An actual reduction of blood and tissue temperature lowers the excretion of carbonic acid and nitrogen." Towards the end of a bath then, and especially during the period immediately following it, febrile combustion of the

86

tissues is reduced, and it is probable that this reduction more than balances the initial increase.

But, while laying proper stress upon the influence of reduction of temperature in limiting the disintegration of nitrogenous and non-nitrogenous substances, it must not be forgotten that the bath-treatment acts in many other directions towards maintaining the body weight. The appetite and digestive power have both been shown to be, comparatively speaking, preserved; the actual circulation of the blood through the tissues is hastened, through the maintenance of the general vascular pressure; and finally the quality of the blood itself is improved. Winternitz has quite recently demonstrated that cold immersion, followed by proper reaction, leads to—(1) an increase in the number of leucocytes; (2) an increase in the percentage of hæmoglobin; and (3) an increase in the specific gravity of the blood. All this tends strongly in the direction of improving the nutrition of the organs and tissues, and thus diminished disintegration is accompanied by increased assimilation.

A not unimportant point in this connexion is the power, already alluded to, which the treatment has to moderate diarrhœa; for under few conditions is loss of body-weight more rapid than in the presence of this symptom, if it be at all severe.

A further question is opened up by Winternitz's discovery of the increased *leucocytosis* following cold-bathing. If it is true, as recently stated, that the microbicidal power of the blood resides mainly in the white corpuscles, then it may become justifiable to assign to the bath-treatment a less indirect action on the specific factor in the disease than has hitherto been claimed for it by its supporters.

Cutaneous Symptoms

The cutaneous structures share with the other tissues in the benefits derived from the bath-treatment. Under systematic bathing the cleanliness and nutrition of the integuments are well preserved, so that it is rare to find the marked dryness and harshness of the skin, or the hide-bound condition not infrequently met with in the later stages of the fever, under ordinary treatment; instead it remains soft, supple, and movable, the subcutaneous tissues being fairly nourished.

Sweating, which is a not uncommon symptom under expectancy, and one which, according to Murchison, is not usually followed by any relief to symptoms, is almost never observed under cold-bathing. This may account in part for the increased diuresis observed, as it certainly does account for the absence of sudamina.

88

With regard to the specific *eruption*, Brand declares that it is less frequent; other observers affirm that its appearance is favoured. No one seems to think that the treatment is absolutely without influence in this respect; yet this would certainly appear to be the most probable alternative.

Hæmorrhagic eruptions are rare in typhoid under any treatment. When they occur, it is in the later stages, or in cases with profound disorganisation of the blood. Systematic refrigeration, by maintaining the power of the circulation, the nutrition of the tissues, and the quality of the blood, has undoubtedly rendered their occurrence less frequent, They are now noticed only in cases that are admitted very late in the fever, or in which some accident or complication has necessitated the suspension of the treatment.

This is also true of *bedsores.* Almost the only cases where these have occurred, leaving out of consideration cases admitted in the advanced typhoid state, have been where perforation or intestinal hæmorrhage have called for a cessation of the bathing, together with the rigid maintenance of the supine position.

Dry gangrene of the extremities from arterial occlusion is extremely rare in any circumstances. I have seen it only twice myself, once under expectancy and once under the bath-treatment. In

89

the latter case three toes were lost; the gangrene was preceded by considerable pain in the parts during and after the baths; and the cutaneous arterial constriction seemed to be excessive. I am inclined to think that systematic rubbing of the parts might have prevented the occurrence.

There is one condition of the skin, described by MM. Tripier and Bouveret, which is undoubtedly due to the action of the baths, namely, *erythematous patches*, accompanied by slight swelling of the subcutaneous tissues, often with tingling and sometimes with articular and muscular pains. They are observed on the extremities, the nose and ears, and are most pronounced after the bath when reaction is setting in; later on they disappear. They are attributed to a transient paralysis of the peripheral vessels of the skin, due to previous over-stimulation of the vaso-constrictors by the action of cold. In Brisbane they do not seem to have been so common as at Lyons, probably on account of the higher average temperature of the water used, and the consequent diminution of the arterial spasm induced. When present, however, they are quite unmistakable. They possess no serious significance.

CHAPTER IV

THE INFLUENCE OF THE TREATMENT UPON THE
DURATION OF THE DISEASE AND UPON THE
OCCURRENCE OF RELAPSES

Duration.—Most authorities agree that the influence of the treatment upon the actual duration of the disease is practically *nil*. This has been the experience of the Brisbane Hospital, provided of course the statement is applied only to cases that convalesce.

Of 373 convalescent cases in the "shorter expectant period," in which the date of fever on admission was tolerably certain, the average duration was 24·0 days.

Of 966 in the three years' "bath period," similarly circumstanced, the average duration was 23·3 days.

The difference, which is very small, may be neglected for the present.

MM. Tripier and Bouveret think that at times the effect of the treatment is to abbreviate the course of the fever itself; but in this view I believe they stand alone. They base their opinion on the observation of two cases that were bathed systematically and rigorously from an unusually early period of the fever. In the first the temperature was high and extremely obstinate, so that the baths had to be reduced to 59° F. to be of any effect. Convalescence, however, set in on the sixteenth day. In the second the temperature was equally high and obstinate; convalescence began on the fourteenth day, but eleven days later a relapse occurred which lasted twelve days.

They argue that in both cases the severity of the symptoms foreshadowed an attack of long duration, and they attribute the early crisis to the uncompromising manner in which the treatment was carried on.

No doubt, as a general rule, cases presenting extreme obstinacy of temperature in the early stages last at least three weeks, yet exceptions are not infrequent. Prior to the introduction of the bath-treatment, not a few cases were seen in the Brisbane Hospital which presented high continuous temperatures, rapid pulse, early delirium, and other symptoms of grave omen, but which terminated by crisis at the end of the second week. Excepting the rash these cases accorded more closely with the classical description of typhus than with that of enteric. There is no reason to believe, therefore, that in the two cases alluded to the duration of the fever was shortened ; on the contrary, it would seem more probable that it was in a sense prolonged, since cases of this nature, when abandoned to expectancy, not uncommonly die before the crisis has had time to arrive. From this point of view it seems probable that some of the cases which formerly succumbed early in the attack to severe pyrexia or hyperpyrexia would have turned out to be abortive had life been sufficiently prolonged.

If now inquiry be made into the duration of the fever in fatal cases, a real influence is found to be exerted.

Of 45 fatal cases in the "shorter expectant period," in which the date of fever on admission was tolerably certain, the average duration was 22·1 days.

Of 68 similarly circumstanced in the three years' "bath period," the average duration was 28·3 days.

There was therefore under the latter treatment an average prolongation of life amounting to 6·2 days. The difference is considerable, but it becomes even greater if we strike out from both series those cases that were fatal from hæmorrhage and perforation, over which the bath-treatment will be shown to exert no influence whatever.

Thus of 26 cases in the "expectant period" which

were fatal from causes other than hæmorrhage and perforation, and in which the date of fever on admission was tolerably certain, the average duration was 22·4 days; while 28 similarly circumstanced in the "bath period" lasted on the average 33·6 days.

There was therefore in this class of fatal cases an average prolongation of life amounting to 11·2 days.

These figures are probably too high; and the data from which they are drawn are certainly numerically small. A more correct idea as to the power of the treatment to prolong life in fatal cases will be gained when dealing with the duration of the stay in hospital.

While it is true that the duration of the fever itself is not curtailed, yet the period of illness as a whole is undoubtedly shortened. This period is made up of the period of fever and that of convalescence. Owing to the influence of cold-bathing in minimising the injurious effects of the pyrexial process, the latter is comparatively rapid, as indeed might have been anticipated.

The period of convalescence is of course difficult to fix definitely; but in order to compare the results of the two treatments in this respect, it will suffice to take the duration of the stay in the hospital; patients being usually discharged only when they were considered fit to take an approximately normal diet, and when it seemed probable that in the course of a week or two they would be able to resume some sort of employment.

During the "shorter expectant period," of 491 cases, the average stay in hospital was 35·9 days.

During the three years' "bath period," of 1033 cases, the average stay was 31·6 days.

There was therefore an average saving in hospital-treatment of 4·8 days; and since it has been shown that the duration of the fever was not appreciably shortened, it follows that this saving was altogether effected out of the period of convalescence.

As Jürgenson says, however, it is really quite unnecessary to prove statistically this shortening of the period of convalescence, since no one who has watched a few cases could have any doubt upon the matter.

It has already been shown that the duration of the fever in fatal cases is prolonged; it goes without saying therefore that their stay in hospital is prolonged. Still, I append the following figures, which, though they prove nothing new, are drawn from more numerous and accurate data than those relating to the duration of the fever, and are therefore of greater statistical value.

Of 85 fatal cases in the "shorter expectant period," the average stay in hospital was 15 days.

Of 141 in the "bath decade," it was 19 days. The average prolongation of life was therefore four days. This difference is of course accentuated by excluding, from both series, cases that died from hæmorrhage and perforation. If we do this we find that—

Of 57 in the "expectant period," the average stay in hospital was 15·3 days.

Of 64 in the "bath decade," it was 23·3 days. Life, in cases that died from causes other than hæmorrhage and perforation, was thus prolonged by eight days on the average.

In short, it would appear that there is no evidence to show that the natural course of the specific fever is in any way interfered with, except in cases in which its tendency is towards death; any abbreviation of the duration of the temperature in convalescent cases is accounted for by the comparative absence of complications and sequelæ. These not infrequently prolong the period during which the temperature is raised above the normal, yet such secondary pyrexia is manifestly not of the specific typhoid nature.

Relapses

Whether the frequency of relapses is increased or diminished by the bath-treatment is another much-debated question. Brand is of opinion that it is diminished. MM. Tripier and Bouveret differ: they quote the statistics of Murchison (2591 cases, 80 relapses), Gerhardt (4434 cases, 280 relapses), and Liebermeister (861 cases, 64 relapses), which yield a total of 7886 cases, with 324 relapses. The percentage of relapses is thus 4·106, and this figure, drawn as it is from so large a number of cases, collected in different countries and epidemics, they regard as *exactly* expressing the frequency of relapses among patients treated in the ordinary way.

With this they compare 2939 cases collected by Brand from various sources, but all treated by the bath-treatment; among these there were 134 relapses, a percentage of 4·56. They consequently conclude that the treatment has an influence tending slightly to increase the frequency of relapses.

Do the facts, however, warrant this conclusion? The percentage of relapses in the two series differs by less than 0·4; does this difference justify any conclusion at all being based upon it?

Newsholme, in his work on *Vital Statistics*, p. 294, says—

" There is unfortunately nothing more common in medical literature than a crude generalisation from insufficient data, especially as to the treatment of disease, ignoring the mathematical rule that the relative values of two or more series are as the square roots of the numbers of observations; so that by increasing the number of observations in any inquiry, the accuracy increases as the square root of the number. The *results obtained even from a large number of observations are, however, only an approximation to the truth,* although the limits of error are reduced with each increase in the number of observations."

It is necessary therefore to find the possible limits of error contained in the above two percentages of relapses. Applying Poisson's formula, we find that, in the first series of cases treated by ordinary means, the true percentage of relapses might vary between 4·7 and 3·5; while in the second the possible variation is even greater, being represented by the figures 5·6 and 3·4. Combining the two series, it is evident that the relapse-rate might vary from 5·6 per cent. in the second to 3·5 in the first, a possible variation of 2·07. Manifestly then, the difference between the two series (0·4 per cent.) is well within the limits of the possible variation, and consequently no conclusion as to the influence of the treatment can be based upon it; paucity of data alone being more than sufficient to account for the apparent discrepancy.

Besides this, however, there are other sources of fallacy involved, and particularly one, namely the incomparability of the data. In order to compare correctly the two series, it is necessary to define strictly the meaning of the word *relapse*, and to be assured that the definition has been rigidly adhered to by each of the observers who are responsible for the data. But on examination it will be found highly improbable that such has been the case.

MM. Tripier and Bouveret define a relapse as a return of the fever at the beginning of convalescence after some days of complete apyrexia, a return which brings with it a certain number of the typhoid symptoms, and is accompanied with a fresh eruption of the rash. Now on looking over a large number of charts, it will be found that some relapses commence as long after the commencement of convalescence as a fortnight or more; some after a week or less; others on the day of convalescence; and others again before the termination of the first attack, during the period of lysis. The two attacks may, in fact, overlap to any extent, so that it may be quite impossible to separate them; and one is driven to conclude that a relapse may occur at any time after or before convalescence. At any rate nothing but an altogether arbitrary line of demarcation divides the so-called true relapse, which is separated from the primary fever by an apyretic interval, from the intercurrent relapse. Now there is nothing to show that, in the

99

two series quoted, this arbitrary line has always been drawn in exactly the same place. It is indeed almost impossible to believe that such should have been the case.

Accepting the definition of a true relapse as a second attack of fever separated from the primary fever by an apyretic interval, *i. e.* by an interval of at least one day, during the whole of which the temperature was below 99° in the rectum, the records of the Brisbane Hospital, during the first two and a half years of the "bath period," show 46 relapses out of 999 cases. This is a relapse rate of 4·6 per cent., almost exactly the same as that noticed by Brand; but if the maximum temperature of the apyretic interval be raised by one degree Fahrenheit, the number of relapses would stand at 64.

On the other hand, if it be necessary, to constitute a true relapse, that it be accompanied by a fresh outbreak of rose-spots, then the number of relapses would be reduced considerably below 46.

There is therefore no guarantee that the facts in the two series quoted by MM. Tripier and Bouveret are strictly comparable, and consequently the slight difference observed in the relapse-rates may be neglected; or rather, it seems to me, it should be accepted as tolerably conclusive evidence that the bath-treatment exercises no influence whatever upon the frequency of relapses.

This is probably the best place to allude to the wide-spread belief among the profession, that cases of relapse are very rarely fatal. So confident are MM. Tripier and Bouveret as to the ultimate recovery of all cases of relapse, that they, otherwise most uncompromising advocates of cold-bathing, advise simple expectancy in regard to the treatment of such cases.

Experience in Brisbane is not confirmatory of the general opinion. Of the 46 cases of true relapse that occurred amongst the 999 cases admitted during the first two-and-a-half years of the "bath period," four died, a mortality per hundred relapses of 8·7. This is slightly higher than the mortality of the whole period; but if we include the cases already alluded to, in which the temperature between the two attacks never quite reached the normal, and thus raise the number of relapses to 64, the mortality rises to 12·5 per cent. of the total.

Of course it is absurd to estimate a percentage from 46 or even from 64 cases, and herein lies the difficulty of determining statistically the true mortality of relapses. In calculating the mortality of the whole disease, it is shown that it is not until we deal with groups of 600 or more consecutive cases that the probable error becomes so small as to be negligible. But to obtain this number of relapses, we should require probably twenty times the number of cases, and there is not to my knowledge in existence so long a list, recorded with sufficient carefulness.

The general belief in the absence of danger in relapses would appear to have risen in some such way as this. *À priori,* it was to be anticipated that relapses would be very largely more fatal than primary attacks, considering the exhausted state of the patient at their onset; but experience showed that this was not so. The discovery that they were considerably less fatal than might have been anticipated, might easily, unless great caution were exercised, have led to the belief that they were actually less fatal than is in reality the case.

That relapses are certainly not less fatal than primary attacks seems certain, and it is most important, both from a prognostic and from a therapeutic point of view, that this should be borne in mind.

CHAPTER V

INFLUENCE OF THE TREATMENT ON MORTALITY AND PROGNOSIS

Mortality

THE death-rate under expectant treatment *plus* cold-sponging, and the occasional use of other refrigerative measures short of the cold bath, from May 15, 1882,[1] to December 31, 1886, a period of nearly five years, averaged 14·8 per cent., and was fairly constant each year.

On January 1, 1887, the bath-treatment was introduced, and has been carried on uninterruptedly down to December 31, 1896, a period of exactly ten years. Tables 1 and 2 contrast the results during the two periods.

Under the bath-treatment, therefore, an improvement has taken place in the Hospital mortality amounting practically to 50 per cent.; in other words, seven out of every hundred cases admitted have

[1] Previous to this date the Hospital-records were inaccurately kept.

TABLE 1.—" *Expectant period.*"

Year.	No. of Cases.	Deaths.	Percentage Mortality.
1882 (from May 15)	147	25	17·0
1883	273	40	14·6
1884	575	89	15·5
1885	369	49	13·3
1886	464	68	14·6
Totals	1828	271	Average 14·8 per cent

TABLE 2.—" *Bath period.*"

Year.	No. of Cases.	Deaths.	Percentage Mortality.
1887	239	27	11·3
1888	339	23	6·8
1889	595	42	7·0
1890	160	16	10·0
1891	137	7	5·1
1892	104	7	6·7
1893	50	2	4·0
1894	79	1	1·3
1895	69	8	11·6
1896	130	10	7·7
Totals	1902	143	Average 7·5 per cent.

been saved by the use of systematic cold-bathing. This result harmonises perfectly with Osler's most recent statement on the subject—" *The cold-bath treatment, rigidly enforced, appears to save from six to eight in each century of typhoid patients admitted to the care of the hospital physician."* [1]

To base a conclusion of this importance upon a bald statement of results is simply to court unfavourable criticism; I shall endeavour, therefore, to show how the fallacies, which tend to inhere in an inquiry of this sort, have been in the present instance sufficiently minimised, if not entirely eliminated. The chief of these arise from—

1. Paucity of data.

2. Variations in the extension of the term typhoid.

3. Variations in the severity of the disease in different countries, climates, and districts, and in different epidemics at the same place; also differences in the age and sex-constitution of the series compared.

4. Errors in diagnosis.

Induction from but a limited number of observations leads to fallacy by allowing chance to exercise a preponderating influence, and thereby to obscure the effects of treatment. This, which is almost a truism, is none the less commonly ignored. To exclude the operation of chance requires a very different number of observations in different diseases. Roughly speaking, the number varies inversely with the standard mortality of the

[1] *Johns Hopkins' Hospital Reports,* Baltimore 1895.

disease. In acute traumatic tetanus, an almost invariably fatal affection, a very few successful cases would be enough. With a disease whose standard mortality is 50 per cent., the list would have to be considerably extended; while in the case of typhoid, in which the majority attacked recover under any treatment, or even in spite of treatment that is positively bad, a very large number of cases is required. It is necessary to have a clear idea as to this minimum number.

In the following Table, 1800 cases admitted between May 15, 1882, and December 12, 1896, whose average mortality was 14·9 per cent., are divided into groups of various sizes, each being consecutive in the order of admission.

TABLE 3.

No. and size of Groups.	Extreme Percentage Mortalities.	Variation
18 consecutive groups of 100 each	8 and 22	14·0
9 ,, ,, 200 ,,	12·5 and 19	6·5
6 ,, ,, 300 ,,	13·3 and 16·3	3·0
3 ,, ,, 600 ,,	14·3 and 15·3	1·0

Since all these cases were submitted to the expectant plan, it may fairly be assumed that the variations in death-rates are independent of treatment, and due almost solely to the intervention of chance.

It is plain, therefore, (*a*) that in the smaller groups the natural variation in mortality is so great that the effects of treatment would be completely obscured; (*b*) that the variation rapidly diminishes as the groups increase in size; and (*c*) that in groups of 600 or more, the probable error is insignificant.

The possible error is, however, much larger. It is to be determined by the second half of Poisson's formula.[1] Tested in this way the "expectant" group of 1828 cases shows a possible error of 2·3 per cent. in its death-rate; the "bath" group of 1902, one of 1·7 per cent. only.

Variations in the extension of the term typhoid have been shown by Liebermeister to be an important source of fallacy. The inclusion in typhoid tables of the milder and indefinite varieties of fever (febricula, simple continued fever, etc.), is a recent, and to some extent a justifiable tendency. Yet for statistical purposes it is evident that some definite standard is required. Great difficulty was at first experienced on this score in regard to classification. Diarrhœa, meteorism, abdominal symptoms, and even the rash, were not infrequently noted to be absent, even in cases where the diagnosis was

---

[1] $\sqrt{\dfrac{2mn}{\mu^3}}$ where μ = the total number of cases; m = the number of deaths; and n = the number of recoveries. (*Vital Statistics*, by A. Newsholme.)

subsequently verified by post-mortem examination.

Again, many cases that came from houses containing patients suffering from undoubted typhoid were so short in their duration, and so mild, as to accord more with the classical description of febricula. Finally, it was determined to take the duration of the pyrexia as the basis for classification. This was found to eliminate the influence of personal bias from the statistics better than any other method.

Accordingly, from the " shorter expectant period " (August 1, 1885, to December 31, 1886, 586 cases, 85 deaths, mortality 14·5 per cent.) previously referred to as personally recorded, all those cases that convalesced before the tenth day of the fever (which all recovered) have been excluded from the typhoid list and separately classed as febricula, although undoubtedly the majority were due to the specific poison, and many were bathed.

Exactly the same system of classification was adopted during the first three years of the " bath period " (1173 cases, 92 deaths, mortality 7·8 per cent.). During the succeeding seven years, however, the term typhoid has apparently been used in an even more restricted sense, resulting in a considerably higher percentage of exclusions. Thus, while 89, or 13·18 of the whole, have been excluded from the "shorter expectant period," 616, or nearly 25 per cent. of the whole, have been excluded from the 1902 cases in the "bath decade."

It is fair to assume, then, that during the latter period no greater extension was allowed to the term.

The definition of the term typhoid here adopted is, of course, purely arbitrary, and most of the advantages attaching to it would accrue from the use of any definition having a duration-basis. Thus four degrees of extension might conveniently be made—

(1) Including all cases usually termed typhoid, simple continued fever, febricula, etc.;

(2) Excluding cases that convalesced before the tenth day;

(3) Excluding cases that convalesced before the fifteenth day;

(4) Excluding cases that convalesced before the twentieth day; and always including all fatal cases.

Applying these to the "shorter expectant period," and to the first three years of the "bath period," we obtain the following Table.

TABLE 4.

Periods.	Degree of Extension.	Cases.	Deaths.	Percentage Mortality.	No. of Cases excluded.	Their percentage of the total.
August 1, 1885, to December 31, 1886 (Expectancy)	1	675	85	12·59	0	0·00
	2	586	85	14·50	89	13·18
	3	515	85	16·50	160	23·70
	4[1]	423	85	20·09	252	37·33
January 1, 1887, to December 31, 1889 (Bath) ...	1	1374	92	6·69	0	0·00
	2	1173	92	7·84	201	14·63
	3	990	92	9·29	384	27·95
	4[1]	772	92	11·92	602	43·81

In compiling a Table of this nature, absolute accuracy is obviously impossible. The exact day of invasion frequently cannot be fixed, and consequently the duration in such cases must remain somewhat doubtful. Therefore, the better to avoid the unconscious operation of personal bias in favour of the bath-treatment, I have, in dealing with the "expectant period," decided doubtful cases in its

[1] Liebermeister asserts that if we include only cases that have a duration of twenty days and upwards, together with all fatal cases without distinction, the average mortality of typhoid under expectant treatment is 20 per cent. or more; and that by a judicious use of antipyretics this is reduced to about 10. This corresponds fairly with the death-rates of the fourth degree of extension in the Table.

favour, but with the "bath period" adversely. The result of this is seen in the last column, where, for each corresponding degree of extension, a higher percentage of exclusions has been made from the "bath period." Further correction would, therefore, tell in favour of the latter.

From this Table it may be concluded—

(1) That the mortality varies so widely with the extension of the term typhoid, that unless this is strictly defined statistics lose much of their value;

(2) That whichever of the four degrees of extension be adopted, the case for the bath-treatment is in no way weakened; and

(3) That no matter how unfairly the "bath period" be treated, if, for instance, the mortality of its fourth degree of extension be compared with that of the first degree of the "expectant period," there still remains a balance in its favour.

For several reasons, however, it has been found most convenient to select for general use the definition involved in the second degree. Murchison more than once alludes to cases lasting only ten days, nor is there any reason to think that such cases were excluded from his statistics. Besides, a classification on this basis appears to accord very nearly with that in use at the Brisbane Hospital in former years, and at the present time in the other large hospitals of Australasia. By its adoption, therefore, wider and more accurate comparisons can be made.

The possible variations in the severity of the disease, owing to climate and other local causes, have not, in the present instance, any importance, since all the cases in either series came from the same districts, were subject to the same climatic conditions, and were treated in the same wards.

Sex-constitution varies but slightly from year to year, and in long series is practically identical. Of the 1828 cases expectantly treated, 668, or 36·5 per cent., were females; of the 1902 in the " bath period," 714, or 37·5 per cent., were females.

Age-constitution is of less importance in typhoid than in many other diseases. Only at the two extremes of life is its influence at all considerable, the mortality being lowest under ten and highest over forty. Of the 586 cases in the " shorter expectant period," 1·08 per cent. were under ten, and 4·33 per cent. over forty. Of the 1902 in the " bath period," 0·7 were under ten, and 6·7 over forty. So far as it goes, therefore, age-constitution tells against the " bath period," but practically it may be neglected.

With regard to variations in severity in different epidemics, seasons, etc., it has been argued that the reduced death-rate during the ten years' " bath period " is largely, if not wholly, due to the type of the disease having become milder. Were this true, similar variations should have occurred previously. But it has been shown (Table 3) that such variations occurred only in the less numerous series, disappearing almost entirely in those containing 600 or more.

Similarly, the annual variations in mortality seen in Table 2 ("bath period"), amounting to 10 per cent., are manifestly due to paucity of data, and not to epidemic influence. This can be demonstrated without difficulty.

If from the whole decade we strike out the first six months, during which the treatment was but inefficiently carried out, we have a series of 1731 consecutive cases, extending over a period of nine and a half years, with 122 deaths. If, now, instead of into years, this series is divided into three equal groups of 577 cases each, we obtain the following Table:—

TABLE 5.

Periods.	No. of Cases.	No. of Deaths.	Percentage Mortality.
July 1, 1887, to December 21, 1889	577	42	7·3
February 22, 1889, to October 14, 1890......	577	40	6·9
October 15, 1890, to December 31, 1896 ...	577	40	6·9

The series being sufficiently long to exclude errors due to paucity of data, the variations practically disappear: there is instead, as has been pointed out by Osler, a remarkable uniformity in the result.

Even the fractional excess in the first group is naturally accounted for, without bringing in the theory of alteration in type. The treatment for some time after its inception was not popular; indeed during the first year or so a great deal of opposition on the part of the public was encountered. Nor had the profession at that time given their full adhesion to the system. It follows naturally that included in the first group is a considerably higher percentage of cases admitted late in the disease or moribund; sufficient at any rate to account fully for the slight difference in results.

Probably the strongest argument in favour of the identity of type of the cases included respectively in the "expectant" and in the "bath" series is found on analysing the immediate causes of death. Presently it will be shown that certain complications and accidents, notably intestinal perforation and hæmorrhage, which the bath-treatment could scarcely be expected *à priori* to prevent, have been equally frequent in each period. *In further support of the contention, therefore, it would be necessary to assume that the change of*

114

type was of so selective a nature, that while it greatly reduced the general mortality of the disease, it left the dangers arising from the intestinal lesion unaffected.

Recently it has been suggested that the cessation of immigration into Queensland may account in great part for the reduced case-mortality at the Brisbane Hospital, as it undoubtedly to a great extent accounts for the reduced prevalence of the disease. Immigration, however, did not cease until about the end of 1889, and its evil effects, if any existed, upon case-mortality would persist for some time longer. But by the end of 1889 (Table 2) the reduction of the mortality to 7 per cent. had been already attained, and no further material fall has since occurred.

Errors in diagnosis do not in the case under consideration affect the statistics. The lists were prepared from the diagnoses recorded in the case-books, and these diagnoses were recorded only at the discharge or death of the patient.

The mortality classified according to the immediate or secondary causes of death.—So far the influence on the general mortality only has been considered, but this method is obviously inadequate in dealing with a disease where death threatens from so many directions. The two ever-present dangers are (1) the pyrexia common to all continued fevers, and

115

(2) the intestinal lesion, peculiar to enteric; and to either or both of these most of the deaths might be referred. *A priori* it could hardly be expected that the treatment would influence the latter, at any rate favourably, and it is essential therefore to settle the point statistically.

Unfortunately a difficulty here arises. Death is so frequently due to a co-operation of the pyrexia and the intestinal lesion, that it is manifestly incorrect in many cases to attribute it solely to either. Especially is this so where severe diarrhoea, meteorism, and other abdominal symptoms have coexisted with prolonged high temperature.

There are, however, two modes of death, namely perforation and hæmorrhage, which should properly be regarded as accidents, inasmuch as they are the result of the depth of the ulcer and not of anything in its specific nature. They are at any rate due to the intestinal lesion and to it alone. Consequently, no question of classification need arise to prevent the statistical determination of their relative frequency in the two series.

Of the 586 cases in the " shorter expectant period," 17 died from perforation and 11 from hæmorrhage.[1] Therefore the percentage mortality

[1] The cases here included are those only in which death was plainly the immediate result of hæmorrhage. Cases which during the attack suffered from hæmorrhage, but recovered

(to total cases) of each accident was 2·90 and 1·88 respectively, or together 4·71.

Of the 1902 cases in the " bath decade," 56 died of perforation and 23 of hæmorrhage. The percentage mortality of each, therefore, was 2·9 and 1·2 respectively, or together 4·1.

Hence it is plain (1) that instead of being more common under the bath-treatment, as many have feared, death from these two complications has been actually, though slightly, less frequent; and (2) that the decrease, such as it is, is altogether due to the diminished frequency of fatal hæmorrhage.

It is to be observed that the figures quoted relate to the mortality caused by these accidents and not to the frequency of their occurrence. In the case of perforation, which is almost of necessity fatal, the distinction is without importance; but it is otherwise with hæmorrhage, which there is reason to think has occurred as frequently (though not more so) under the bath-treatment as before. Its diminished mortality is doubtless explicable by the improved general state of the patient at its onset, enabling him to recover the better from the loss of blood.

The conclusion therefore is, that the treatment

from it, to die afterwards from other causes, are classified accordingly.

has no effect upon the occurrence of perforation or hæmorrhage one way or the other, but that it renders the latter slightly less dangerous.

Modes of death other than the above.—Obviously it is among these that the main source of the reduced general mortality must be sought.

During the " shorter expectant period " the deaths under this head were 57 : their mortality relative to total cases being thus 9·73 per cent.

During the " bath decade " they numbered 64, their mortality being therefore 3·4 per cent. Death from this group of causes is thus hardly more than one-third as frequent under cold-bathing.

Now some of the causes of death in this list are well defined and undoubtedly " pyrexial " in origin, inasmuch as they are liable to arise in any severe continued fever. They are—

(*a*) Chest affections, *e. g.* pneumonia, empyema, etc. ; simple hypostatic congestion of the lungs is not here included.

(*b*) Cerebral affections, *e. g.* acute mania, general convulsions, apoplexy, etc.

The remainder may for the present be grouped together under the head of—

(*c*) Exhaustion. Table 6 contrasts the " shorter expectant period " with the first three years of the " bath period."

TABLE 6.

Classes.	"Expectant period," 586 cases.		"Bath period," 1173 cases.	
	Deaths.	Percentage Mortality.	Deaths.	Percentage Mortality.
(a) Chest	13	2·22	6	0·51
(b) Cerebral	4	0·68	2	0·17
(c) Exhaustion, etc.	40	6·83	34	2·9
Totals	57	9·73	42	3·58

(a) Fatal chest-affections have thus been less than one-fourth as frequent. Of the six in the "bath period," one was from empyema, which became chronic and proved fatal six months after the subsidence of the fever; three from acute lobar pneumonia, in all of which the complication developed suddenly and rapidly carried off the patient; and two only from broncho-pneumonia, in one of which it was present on admission, and led to a wrong diagnosis (acute tuberculosis).

In only one instance, then, did fatal broncho-pneumonia develop subsequently to admission.

It is doubtful how many of the thirteen deaths attributed to chest-affections in the "expectant period" were due to this variety of pneumonia, but certainly a majority were so caused. The greater success attained in averting broncho-pneumonia by cold-bathing is in accord with what is known of the pathology of the disease, and has already been referred to.

(*b*) The deaths in this class are only those in which some well-marked cerebral complication developed at a time when as yet no other threatening symptoms had appeared; in which death rapidly followed ; and in which therefore it is fair to assume that it proceeded chiefly, if not solely, from the brain. These were cases of acute mania, general convulsions, apoplexy from subarachnoid hæmorrhage, and one unusual case of coma.

Although the mortality in this class is seen to have fallen to exactly one-quarter, yet the cases are too few to be in themselves conclusive. Better evidence as to the influence of cold-bathing on the nervous system has already been adduced in discussing the nervous symptoms of the disease.

(*c*) The mortality of this class is seen to have been reduced from 6·82 per cent. to 2·89 ; or by nearly 58 per cent. The class constitutes, as has already been said, a residuum. In it are included most of the causes of death termed pyrexial, together with others due to the intestinal lesion. No accurate comparison, however, between the two periods can be instituted for two reasons—(1) because the distinction between the influence of the lesion and that of the pyrexia is not always sharply defined ;

120

and (2) because during the " expectant period " the record was not sufficiently minute.

I propose, however, to analyse the thirty-four cases included in the " bath period," pointing out as far as possible the respective influence of the two above-mentioned factors on the mortality.

To begin with, some cases hardly bear upon the question of treatment at all : three cases were fatal from abortion (septicæmia 2, flooding 1), in two of which the accident preceded admission ; in five death was due to altogether exceptional causes, or was clearly dependent on pre-existing disease. These comprised pyæmia, parotid bubo, old fatty heart, acute cystitis, and urethral stricture with general disorganisation of the urinary organs.

In twelve the intestinal lesion seemed to be the most important factor. In three, exhaustion appeared to be the immediate result of profuse diarrhœa. This certainly contrasts favourably with the " expectant period," when this symptom was no uncommon cause of death. In the remaining nine the fatal exhaustion was due undoubtedly to dysentery. In most the patient was convalescent, or nearly so, at the time of its onset, and in all extensive ulceration of the rectum, sigmoid flexure, or both, was found *post mortem.*

There yet remained fourteen cases in which no special cause for death, in addition to the fever, could be discovered, and in which the fatal event must therefore be attributed to "simple pyrexial cardiac failure." These are the cases which without any substantive complications, or at any rate with only such as are directly due to a failing circulation (*e. g.* general hypostasis, bedsores, etc.), slowly or rapidly, according to the intensity of the pyrexia, fall into the typhoid state and succumb.

Now this is the mode of death which of a certainty during the "expectant period" accounted for a larger share in the general typhoid death-rate than any other group of causes ; and therefore it may be said unhesitatingly, that it is above all in preventing this kind of fatality that the bath-treatment is efficacious.

In further support of this statement, it will be found that most of the fourteen cases in this group were admitted in circumstances that were highly unfavourable.

Thus four were practically moribund on admission, and died in less than 72 hours; four were admitted during the fourth week of the disease or later ; two during the third ; two during the second ; and two only before the end of the first. The significance of this analysis will be appreciated when it is known that more than 53 per cent. of the total cases were admitted during the first week of the disease.

If it were allowed to make an approximate estimate of the relative percentages of this mode of death, in the two periods, I should say that it had fallen from about five in the former to a little above one in the latter.

Influence of Delayed Admission.—It is admitted by all that delay in seeking admission has a baneful influence upon the hospital death-rate of typhoid. This has been noticed incidentally in referring to Table 5. It has not, however, been generally recognised that the increased mortality attending cases admitted late in the disease is almost wholly due to the greater number that die from causes other than hæmorrhage and perforation. This at any rate was found to be the case during the "expectant period" at the Brisbane Hospital.

A fortiori the same must be true of the "bath period," since the treatment has been proved to be mainly "antipyrexial."

Table 7 shows the cases admitted during the three years' "bath period," omitting the first six months, arranged into two classes—(1) Those admitted on the eighth day of the fever or earlier; (2) those admitted later, together with their respective general and special mortalities.

TABLE 7.

Classes.	No. of Cases.	Died of Perforation and Hæmorrhage.	Percentage Mortality to Total Cases.	Died from Other Causes.	Percentage Mortality to Total Cases.	General Mortality.
(1) Admitted on the eighth day of the fever or earlier.	552 [1]	22	3·98	10	1·81	5·79
(2) Admitted later than the eighth day of fever.	401 [1]	16	3·99	23	5·73	9·72

Thus it appears that—

(1) Delayed admission was practically without influence in increasing the danger of death from perforation or hæmorrhage; and

[1] Forty-nine cases, in which it was impossible to say whether they were admitted before or after the eighth day, are omitted. These all recovered. Probably an objection may be made to this Table (and to Table 8) on the ground that in many cases the invasion of typhoid is so insidious that it is impossible to fix the exact day of onset. A little consideration, however, will show that this objection does not apply with any force to fixing the week in which the fever began, which is in fact all that has been here attempted.

(2) The whole difference in mortality in favour of cases admitted early was due to the lessened mortality from causes mainly pyrexial in nature.

Sex Mortality.—Murchison found the female death-rate to be rather higher than the male; but he observed that this was in spite of the undoubted fact that perforation was considerably more common in males. Its relative frequency he put at 2·3 to 1. He does not appear to have remarked that the same was true of fatal hæmorrhage.

It would appear that while males are more liable than females to succumb to the intestinal lesion, the reverse is the case in an even greater degree with regard to the pyrexia.

It might be anticipated, therefore, with some confidence, that the bath-treatment would influence more favourably the female than the male mortality.

During the whole period of expectancy 1160 males and 668 females were admitted. Of the former 164 died, a mortality of 14·14 per cent.; of the latter 107, a mortality of 16·02 per cent. So that up to the introduction of the bath-treatment on January 1, 1887, the respective death-rates of the two sexes differed but slightly from what had been observed by Murchison.

In striking contrast to this are the results obtained during the "bath decade." During this period 1188 males and 714 females were admitted. Of the former 103 died, a mortality of 8·7 per cent. ; of the latter 40, a mortality of 5·6 per cent. ; so that while the male death-rate fell from 14·14 per cent. to 8·7, a reduction of 38 per cent., the female was reduced from 16·02 to 5·6, or a reduction of 65 per cent.

That the greater success experienced with female patients is almost entirely due to their comparative immunity from the two intestinal accidents can be readily demonstrated.

Of the 40 female fatal cases, 14 died from perforation and 6 from hæmorrhage. The percentage mortality (to women admitted) of the two accidents was therefore 1·9 and 0·8 respectively, or together 2·7.

Of the 103 male fatal cases, perforation accounted for 42 and hæmorrhage for 17 deaths ; and the percentage mortality (to males admitted) was therefore 3·5 and 1·4 respectively, or together 4·9.

Death from either accident was thus almost twice as frequent in the male sex.

Subtracting the fatal cases here specified from the total deaths in either sex, it is found that causes of death other than perforation and hæmorrhage are more frequent in males (3·7 per cent.) than females (2·8 per cent.).

The difference, which does not amount to 1 per

cent. of the cases admitted, is probably to be explained, in part at any rate, by the more frequent occurrence of hæmorrhage in men, which is included in these numbers when it was only a contributory cause of death.

It has been shown that delayed admission has but little effect in augmenting the mortality from perforation and hæmorrhage. This fact, taken in conjunction with the fact that males are much more liable to these accidents, seems to point to the inference that early admission is relatively of more importance in the female wards.

An appeal to figures is confirmatory of this surmise, as is seen in the annexed Table.

TABLE 8.

Classes according to Date of Admission.	No. of Cases.	MALES.			FEMALES.		
		No. of Deaths.	Percentage Mortality.	No. of Cases.	No. of Deaths.	Percentage Mortality.
Admitted on the eighth day or earlier.	404	34	8·42	229	5	2·18
Admitted later than the eighth day.	290	35	12·07	181	18	9·94

The cases here included are those of the first three years of the " bath period," *minus* sixty-nine (who all recovered), in which it was found impossible to determine the week of the fever on admission. Thus while the mortality of males admitted during the first week was about 30 per cent. lower than the mortality of those admitted later, the female death-rate under the same conditions was less by 78 per cent.

The explanation is evident. Analysing the five deaths that occurred among the 229 females admitted during the first week of the disease, three are found to have died of perforation, and the other two from dysentery, Death from purely pyrexial causes was therefore entirely absent from this group.

The series of 1902 cases treated during the " bath decade" in the Brisbane Hospital include every case admitted during the term which at its termination was diagnosed as typhoid, omitting only twenty-three cases still under treatment when the statistics were compiled. It includes therefore many cases that were not bathed at all, because such treatment was contra-indicated; many more that were not bathed because the pyrexia was insufficiently high to require it under Brand's rule; many that were hopeless on admission; some that died from old-standing or intercurrent diseases, during the course of an attack of typhoid; and some that were diagnosed only at the necropsy. The death-rate therefore is essentially a hospital typhoid death-rate, and should not be confounded, as it frequently is, with the probable death-rate in cases appropriate to the treatment.

Prognosis

It follows naturally from the preceding that the prognosis under cold-bathing is at any rate 50 per cent. better than under expectancy; but while the prognosis has improved, it has also greatly altered, so as to merit an entire reconsideration. Conditions such as sex and date of fever on admission, and also many symptoms and complications, have changed materially in prognostic value.

Sex, which under expectancy might almost be neglected in framing a prognosis, has come to occupy a position of great importance. For instance, in any two given cases of opposite sexes, *ceteris paribus*, and without reference to the date of fever on admission, the danger to life in the female is but two-thirds that in the male; while if both are admitted during the first week of the fever, the difference becomes exaggerated.

Delayed admission, always unfavourable, is under the bath-treatment relatively more unfavourable

129   K

than before; that is to say, cases lose more by
delay in seeking admission under the bath-treatment than under expectancy, since the former
is active to avert the progressively-increasing
danger of continued pyrexia.

Many symptoms which were formerly of most
serious import have fallen considerably in value
from a prognostic point of view, while others,
though not actually more indicative of a fatal issue,
have come to occupy a more prominent place in
the mortality list. The latter consideration refers
especially to intestinal hæmorrhage and perforation,
accidents which, as already mentioned, depend
upon the tendency which the ulceration has in
some cases to penetrate deeply towards the peritoneal surface.

The causes which lead to this tendency are, so
far as I am aware, quite unknown; treatment does
not modify the tendency, nor can it be foreseen.
It is true that Jenner long ago averred that muscular
tremors, occurring in patients whose mental faculties
remained clear, indicated deep ulceration; and this
statement has been copied into text-books down to
the present day. There seems no *à priori* reason
why this should be the rule, and my own experience is not confirmatory of it. On the contrary,
deep ulceration as indicated by perforation and
hæmorrhage has been common under the bath-

treatment, muscular tremors extremely rare, occurring only in cases with advanced prostration.

Both accidents are rather more frequent in cases where there has been diarrhœa, but not rarely they have followed absolute constipation. Of twenty-eight cases of perforation, in six there had been constipation, in seven regular loose motions, in eleven diarrhœa, and in four very severe diarrhœa. Of thirteen cases of fatal hæmorrhage, in six there had been regular loose motions, in four diarrhœa, and in three very severe diarrhœa. The possibility of the occurrence of either accident must therefore always be borne in mind in forming a prognosis in all cases, no matter how mild, except those of the shortest duration.

Perforation is of course nearly always fatal under this as under any other form of medical treatment. As already seen, it is neither more nor less liable to occur under the bath-treatment than under expectancy; but owing to the diminished number of deaths from other causes, it occupies a more important position in the mortality-list. Murchison states that perforation occurred in 3 per cent. of all his cases, and in 20 per cent. of the fatal ones. In Brisbane during the " expectant period " it occurred in 2·90 per cent. of all cases, and in exactly 20 per cent. of the fatal ones. During the " bath decade," however, while it occurred in exactly the same percentage of all cases (2·90), its percentage rate to fatal cases rose to nearly 40.

Hæmorrhage has been shown to be a slightly less frequent cause of death under the bath-treatment; yet like perforation it has become a more important item in the list of fatal cases. While its mortality, per hundred cases admitted, fell from 1·88 in the "expectant period" to 1·2 in the "bath period," its percentage-rate to fatal cases rose from nearly 13 to over 16.

Much difference of opinion exists as to the significance of intestinal hæmorrhage; some observers appearing to regard it as beneficial at times, while the majority look upon it as invariably of grave import. Personally I have never seen a case where I could assure myself that it had contributed to recovery; although in several a single attack has coincided with the natural defervescence. Considering that the accident, which may occur at almost any period of the disease, is especially likely during the period of slough-separation, *i.e.* at the time when convalescence may be expected, it would be strange indeed if this did not occasionally happen.

The occurrence of intestinal hæmorrhage in an average case of typhoid renders the prognosis vastly more grave. Of eighty-five cases in which it took place during the first three years of the "bath period," thirty died, a mortality of 35·3 per cent., as against a general mortality of 7·8 per cent. The chances of death ensuing are therefore increased at least four-fold. The danger is immediate; of the thirty fatal cases sixteen died from syncope, the direct result of loss of blood; five of these died on the day on which the blood first appeared; seven within three days, and three within seven. The danger is also remote, for since hæmorrhage in quantity always indicates deep ulceration, perforation is especially liable to occur. Of the thirty fatal cases, perforation accounted for death in seven, or in 8·2 per cent. of all the cases in which hæmorrhage occurred.

Neither of these modes of death is in my opinion preventible to any appreciable extent; but what renders the onset of hæmorrhage especially unfortunate is the fact that it necessitates the suspension of bathing, for a time at least, and thereby increases the ultimate danger from pyrexial causes which are otherwise very largely preventible. Thus of the eighty-five cases in which hæmorrhage occurred, 7, or 8·2 per cent., died of causes other than perforation and hæmorrhage. This is more than twice the mortality occasioned by this group of causes, during the three years' "bath period."

Reference is elsewhere made to the rapidity with which cases assume the typhoid state, when the baths are suspended, and the temperature is thereby allowed to run its course unchecked; and also to the extreme difficulty of steering between the two dangers of further hæmorrhage on the one hand and fatal pyrexia on the other.

The other symptoms connected with the intestinal lesion, but not especially due to its depth, namely diarrhœa and meteorism, have already been shown to be more or less prevented or modified by cold-bathing and other methods of external refrigeration. It is consequently rarer for these complications to cause anxiety; but for this reason they are more serious regarded as prognostic indications, when they arise during the course of and persist in spite of the treatment, since it is only the most severe forms which do so. On the other hand, when they are present on admission, unless greatly aggravated, it is always probable that a few days of the treatment will cause them to abate or disappear.

With regard to diarrhœa, the nature and consistence of the motions are better guides to prognosis than their mere frequency; a profuse watery diarrhœa being always of unfavourable import. The dysenteric form of diarrhœa has been found at the Brisbane Hospital to be a most intractable and highly dangerous complication.

Simple high temperature has under the bath-treatment almost ceased to be regarded as of unfavourable import. Under expectancy, even when aided by antipyretic drugs, cases that present a continuously high temperature in the early stages are always looked upon with much apprehension. *Ceteris paribus*, the higher the temperature-range the greater the danger. This does not hold good under the bath-treatment, provided the case comes under notice fairly early, and that *the refrigeration is adequately pushed.* Indeed great resistance to refrigeration, in the early stages, has come to be regarded as almost of favourable import, since cases presenting it usually exhibit no signs of circulatory failure. It is usually to be anticipated, however, that when the resistance to refrigeration is such that the baths have to be reduced to 60° F., and their duration much prolonged, the course of the fever will be protracted—twenty to thirty days at least—and a large number of baths, probably over one hundred, will be required.

Most favourable, from a prognostic point of view, are the cases where the temperature is of moderate intensity, and where baths of ordinary temperature and duration are sufficient to cause the required fall in temperature. Coincident with this, however, there must also be a corresponding amelioration in the other symptoms of pyrexia, more especially in the pulse and in the nervous symptoms. An exception to this may be made in regard to those cases where the pulse-rate is hardly raised above the normal, and in which there is but little room for improvement in this respect. In these cases of moderate fever, after a day or two of treatment, the temperature will often be found to be below bathing-point when the bath is due, so that one or two baths may be missed. This usually, though not by any means always, augurs a shorter duration and milder general symptoms.

An easily-reduced temperature is not, however, *per se* a favourable sign. It has been already stated that, in the later stages of the disease, the temperature is reduced with comparative ease, the reverse being the case with the pulse-rate. This is especially true of cases that come under treatment only in the later stages. In these it is the rule for the temperature to give way rapidly to the bath, but the other symptoms do not abate correspondingly; the pulse remains too frequent, delirium if present persists, and the tongue fails to become appreciably more moist. The temperature falls because the automatic heat-regulating function of the body is impaired, and along with this there is always a considerable degree of circulatory feebleness. The temperature has in these cases worked many of its worst effects which the treatment was especially designed to avert, and consequently the prognosis is unfavourable, although there are few cases indeed that fail to derive some benefit from a continuance of the bathing.

The state of the circulation as determined by an examination of the heart and pulse is probably of more importance in prognosis than any other symptom or group of symptoms. This has always been so, but under the bath-treatment it is an especially good guide, since in addition to its characteristics as ordinarily displayed, we are enabled to observe its behaviour under rapidly-varying conditions of temperature and thermal stimulation. In cases presenting a rapid pulse on admission, a far better estimate of its prognostic value can be made after observing the effect of a few immersions. Cases where a decided fall in the pulse-rate is produced are relatively more favourable than others in which the pulse, though starting from a lower rate, is yet less influenced by the bath. The amount of the fall in the pulse-rate following the bath may in fact be regarded as a measure of the recuperative power of the circulation.

In estimating for the purpose of prognosis the degree of circulatory failure, it is always necessary to take into consideration the tonic and stimulant powers of quinine and alcohol. Unexpectedly-rapid improvement has frequently followed the administration of these drugs, *plus* regular bathing, in cases admitted late in the typhoid state. Twenty-four hours' treatment has not uncommonly altered a quick, irregular, running pulse of 140 to a fairly satisfactory one well below 120; and this without any permanent abatement of the temperature-range.

Mental disturbances of all kinds have been seen to be vastly less common under systematic bathing. They are consequently of more serious import when they arise during its continuance, and especially when they persist in spite of the treatment. One case occurred in which acute delirious mania came on during the first week of the fever; in which bathing served but to excite; and in which death quickly ensued from sheer exhaustion. Such cases are of course extremely rare.

Of no prognostic significance is the occurrence of slight delirium for the first time, when, in accordance with Brand's rule, the falling temperature of approaching convalescence leads to a cessation of the bathing, since in all such cases a short dip, insufficient appreciably to lower the temperature, will immediately clear up the symptom. Quite different, however, is it in cases where delirium follows the cessation of the bathing, when this has been necessitated by the onset of some complication such as intestinal hæmorrhage, for then the most valid method of treatment is contra-indicated.

Stupor on admission, unless very profound or accompanied by other grave symptoms such as great

138

circulatory feebleness, albuminuria, etc., is not necessarily of bad augury. Patients presenting the symptoms not unfrequently become lucid after a day or two of regular treatment by very cold baths of short duration.

The bronchial catarrh, so common at the commencement of the fever, has been shown to be very favourably modified by the treatment. Since it seems probable that it is the primary cause of many fatal cases of broncho-pneumonia, it would follow that it is of much less importance in prognosis under the bath-treatment than under expectancy.

The significance of pneumonia varies widely. When it affects only a small portion of lung-tissue, it may not appreciably alter the pulse-rate and temperature; in this case, therefore, it does not add much to the danger. But sometimes a whole lobe is attacked, rapid heart-failure supervenes, and the case soon becomes hopeless. Every gradation between these two extremes may be met with, and the danger in each case is best estimated by the effect which the complication produces on the temperature and pulse. Generally speaking, the prognosis of pneumonia under the bath-treatment is better than under expectancy.

When, in the early stages of the fever, the urine passed is unusually small in quantity, and of high colour and specific gravity, the case is commonly

139

regarded as likely to be severe. Under the bath-treatment less anxiety need be felt, since this acts as a powerful diuretic. The presence of a small quantity of albumin has never seemed to affect the prognosis, at any rate under the bath-treatment. In some cases it clears up in the course of the bathing, but more commonly it persists till convalescence. Albumin in large quantities of course indicates nephritis, and necessarily renders the prognosis grave.

Improvement in the symptoms in connexion with the upper part of the alimentary canal is of good augury; and naturally their persistence in an unmodified form is the reverse. This applies especially to the buccal and gastric cavities; but it is very easy to lay too much stress upon the condition of the tongue. No doubt it is a good sign when a dry and brown tongue becomes moist and white after each bath, and still more so when it remains in this state through the interval; but the absence of this change does not necessarily indicate any great danger. Some cases go through the greater part of the fever with an obstinately dry and brown tongue, and yet never present any symptoms of nervous prostration or circulatory feebleness.

CHAPTER VI

CONTRA-INDICATIONS — CONDITIONS AND SYMPTOMS
REQUIRING MODIFICATIONS IN THE TREATMENT :
ADDITIONAL THERAPEUTIC PROCEDURES

Contra-indications

CONTRA-INDICATING complications arising during
the course of the disease, and depending on it, are
dealt with in considering the modifications of the
treatment that may become necessary. There are,
however, certain conditions which, though they
rarely form distinct contra-indications, yet merit
some consideration, since by the inexperienced they
might be considered a bar to the treatment.

Some of these are physiological, such as menstruation, pregnancy, the puerperal state and suckling,
old age and childhood. The last two are considered
elsewhere.

On commencing the treatment much hesitation
was felt in continuing its rigid application during *menstruation.* It seemed not improbable that
to plunge a patient in this state into water of

a temperature of 70° F. might at least lead to a sudden checking of the flow, and thus to certain injurious consequences, if not indeed to inflammatory pelvic complications. Accordingly, if the necessity for refrigeration was not urgent, the temperature of the patient being only moderately above the bathing-point, it was the custom to discontinue the baths until the menstrual period was over. In the cases where the temperature was higher, and where consequently to abandon its control for three or four days seemed likely to be fraught with serious consequences, the bathing was continued; but the temperature of the water was raised to 80° or even more. In this way it seemed likely that the shock and the consequent sudden disturbance of the pelvic circulation would be diminished. Immunity from accidents, however, soon led to a tentative reduction in the temperature of the bath-water, which was gradually lowered by a few degrees at a time, so that soon the baths began to be given at the ordinary temperature. This finally became the rule of practice, and although occasionally some slight checking of the flow appeared to follow, the check was not of itself of importance, and certainly no complications or unpleasant symptoms ever resulted.

Pregnancy merits consideration from several points of view—(1) the frequency of abortion;

(2) the maternal mortality; and (3) the fœtal mortality.

My own experience is quite insufficient to throw light on any of these questions; nor do there appear to be any trustworthy data recorded that are sufficiently numerous to do so. With regard to the frequency of abortion, MM. Tripier and Bouveret refer to 108 cases, expectantly treated, with 69 abortions; as against 26 cases treated by cold baths, of which 17 aborted. The percentage of abortions in the two series was therefore 64 and 65 respectively; but it is plain that the difference is so small, and the probable error in each series so large, that no conclusion can be drawn from these figures as to the influence of the treatment.

Some theoretical considerations, however, may be adduced in favour of the bath-treatment. It has been observed, that when the maternal temperature is maintained at 104°, the fœtal heart and also the fœtal movements increase considerably in frequency; the fœtus in fact participates in the pyrexia of the mother. It seems also to be true that abortion is more certain as the temperature is higher and the fever more prolonged. Both facts therefore tend to the conclusion, that in the temperature lies the cause of the death of the fœtus which precedes its premature expulsion; and

143

if this is so, the advantages of the bath-treatment must be provisionally admitted (Tripier and Bouveret). With regard to the maternal mortality, of the 108 cases expectantly treated, 16 died, a percentage of 15; of the 26 cases treated by cold baths, 3 died, a percentage of 11·5. While these figures are quite insufficient to establish the superiority of the bath-treatment, they may be taken to show that it is not fraught with any special danger to pregnant women.

There is nothing in the *puerperal state*, so long as it is purely physiological, to contra-indicate the employment of cold-bathing. The state undoubtedly renders the prognosis more grave, mainly, according to Brand, because the diagnosis of typhoid, always much obscured, is frequently not made until late in the attack.

With regard to *suckling*, I must admit that it never occurred to me to regard it in the light of a possible contra-indication. No bad effects were ever observed in the few cases where lactation was in progress on admission.

It is especially fortunate that none of the physiological conditions peculiar to the female sex constitute contra-indications to cold-bathing, since, as elsewhere shown, women have more to gain than men from the treatment and from submitting to it early and systematically.

The other conditions referred to are pathological, and embrace certain diatheses and pre-existing diseases. It is not infrequently asked whether it is wise to subject a patient with hereditary phthisical tendency to the cold-bath treatment. I do not think it will occur to the next generation of physicians to ask the question; that it is asked at the present time is probably due to the fact that we have not in reality completely rid ourselves of the old ideas as to the pathology of tuberculous affections. Of course a treatment that is liable to cause bronchial catarrh or inflammatory lung-complications would, in the presence of the specific microbe, and especially in a predisposed subject, be liable to lead indirectly to tuberculous disease; but there is ample evidence to show that the bath-treatment does not stand in this position; that in fact bronchial and pneumonic affections are rendered less frequent or are favourably modified under its influence.

Again, should patients with already-developed phthisis or chronic bronchitis, asthmatics, and emphysematous subjects, be exempted from the general rule of bathing? Phthisis in the acute form would, I imagine, generally contra-indicate cold-bathing, mainly on the score of its uselessness; but this does not apply to the chronic forms or to those in which the tuberculous lesion is cured or even quiescent. At Brisbane, during the great immigration years, several patients who had recently been sent to the Colony on account of incipient or chronic phthisis contracted typhoid on arrival, and were treated systematically by cold-bathing without modification of any sort, and with none but the best results.

Chronic bronchitis, emphysema, and asthma do not *per se* contra-indicate the bath-treatment. It must be remembered, however, that all three affections are liable to be complicated in the long run by secondary affections of the right heart. The presence of a flabby dilated heart, although it does not of necessity call for the abandonment of all refrigerative procedures, does entail considerable caution in their employment, so as to avoid shock and sudden strain on the enfeebled organ. Probably the tepid bath or the modification of Ziemssen, carried not too far, is the most suitable form of refrigeration for these cases.

Much the same applies to cases suffering from old valvular lesions of the heart. Many of these patients follow their ordinary occupation for years with practically no symptoms, and with no increase in the physical signs of their complaint. In them, doubtless, compensation is perfect. These bear the ordinary bath-treatment equally well with those who are organically sound. It is otherwise however when compensation is insufficient; when there is palpitation on slight exertion, œdema of the lower extremities, and other signs of commencing circulatory failure. Cold-bathing should not then be used. Tepid baths, or Ziemssen's modification, cautiously tried, are all that we can hope to use with safety. Generally it may be said with regard to these cases, that the kind and amount of refrigeration is better regulated by a consideration of the symptoms and general condition than by the stethoscope alone.

I have treated so far as I know only one case of typhoid suffering from chronic Bright's disease. No baths were used, and the case ended fatally. This affection is not usually regarded as constituting a contra-indication to cold-bathing.

Temperature

The general rule for the administration of the baths has been already stated. It is obvious, however, that in the case of a fever which varies so widely as typhoid, any general rule as to the temperature, duration, and frequency of the baths must have many and important exceptions. Primarily the indication is to *apportion the degree of refrigeration to the intensity of the pyrexia,* and the indication may be fulfilled in several ways.

147

Brand commences by giving a bath of a temperature of 68° F. and of a duration of fifteen minutes, every three hours night and day. Should the fall in temperature not amount to 1·5° F. or 1·8° F., he reduces the temperature of the bath-water straightway to 59° F., because experience has taught him that any reduction short of this does not appreciably increase the antipyretic effect. Others instead of lowering the temperature have prolonged the duration of the bath. Which is the better alternative is a question that is open to argument; in my own case there was but little option. In Brisbane during the summer it was rarely possible to obtain water as low as 70° F., and 59° could only be attained by great expenditure of ice. Consequently, to increase the antipyretic effect in ordinary cases the duration of the bath was gradually prolonged, baths of reduced temperature being reserved for cases of intense pyrexia.

The following definite rule of practice was finally adopted. The first bath is of a temperature of as near 70° F. as possible, and lasts ten minutes. In the event of an insufficient fall in the temperature following, each succeeding bath is prolonged by five minutes, until the desired result is attained. When the bath has reached a duration of thirty or forty minutes, and still fails to reduce the temperature sufficiently, then the temperature of the water is reduced by 5° F. at a time, by the addition of ice, down to 60° F. or even 57°. There are cases, however, in which even this will not suffice, and in them I have again gradually prolonged the duration of the bath to sixty minutes.

Cases which present such extreme resistance to refrigeration are uncommon. The most noticeable instance that occurred in Brisbane was that of a hospital nurse who contracted typhoid in the ward. The following observations taken from the bathing-columns of the record will explain themselves.

		Before bath.				Half-an-hour after bath.	
Day of fever.	Time.	Temperature.	Pulse.	Duration of bath.	Temperature of bath.	Temperature.	Pulse.
5	5.15 p.m.	104·8	120	40 min.	57° F.	104·6	120
	8.30 ,,	103·6	128	40 ,,	,,	103·2	128
	11.30 ,,	104	128	60 ,,	,,	101·8	116
6	2.30 a.m.	103·8	124	60 ,,	,,	100·4	120
	5.30 ,,	103·8	128	60 ,,	,,	102·2	112
	8.30 ,,	102·2	130	60 ,,	,,	102·2	116
	11.30 ,,	103·2	128	60 ,,	,,	102·8	120
	2.30 p.m.	102·8	136	60 ,,	,,	101·8	102
	5.30 ,,	103·2	128	60 ,,	,,	101·6	112

This case did not finally convalesce until the thirty-seventh day of the fever, and needed in all 134 baths, varying in duration from 20 to 60 minutes each.

It is in considering such cases that the conclusions of Winternitz, already alluded to, are of great interest and importance. Winternitz has demonstrated most clearly, that the main resistance to antipyresis by the bath lies primarily in the lessening of the cutaneous circulation, and secondarily in the increased circulation in the muscular layer. It follows naturally that the most appropriate means of overcoming the obstinacy of the temperature is "to maintain constantly the dilatation of the peripheral vessels, before, during, and after the heat-abstraction." To this end he employs frictions and slappings of the surface of the body before and during the bath, and he speaks well as to the result.

For myself, I have proceeded differently. In cases which presented unusual resistance to refrigeration, the baths were steadily reduced in temperature and prolonged in duration, until, as in the case cited, the patient remained for one hour in water below 60° F. During such an apparently severe proceeding, it was usually considered expedient to administer some alcohol, to obviate possible but unknown dangers. Soon it was observed that, in the cases where alcohol was given, the obstinacy of the temperature remitted somewhat; and thenceforward it became the practice to give alcohol with the specific object of assisting the action of the bath, where this latter appeared to be insufficiently powerful. The conclusion thus empirically arrived at seems to be confirmatory of the theory of

Winternitz, for alcohol undoubtedly, among its numerous effects, acts as a vaso-dilator and markedly increases the cutaneous circulation.

There will remain, however, a few isolated cases of obstinate pyrexia in which, through nervousness or some other idiosyncrasy of the patient, it is not possible to push refrigerative measures to the extent mentioned. To these I have been in the habit of administering, in addition, antifebrin. Much has been said, especially by the advocates of cold-bathing, against the use of this drug, and there can be no doubt that it is capable of much injury. Given in too large doses, it has frequently caused severe collapse; given too frequently and for too long a period, it certainly induces a form of anæmia indicated by a somewhat cyanotic pallor of the lips, etc.; but it is quite possible to obtain its beneficial action, and at the same time to avoid any untoward result. It should never be given in doses exceeding five grains for an adult, and its use should be limited strictly to the cases just described; it should be regarded in fact as a *pis aller*. Furthermore, its use should be limited in these cases to the period, usually but a few days, during which the temperature is obstinate, being discontinued immediately the temperature becomes manageable by the bath. Finally, it should not be given more than three times in the twenty-four hours; once is frequently enough. It is hardly necessary to add, that in no circumstances should the drug be regarded in any light but that of an *adjuvant* to the bath. Used with these restrictions, I have never observed any ill effects. On the contrary, it has often occurred that after the administration of one or two doses, the pyrexia has become, at any rate for the time being, amenable to external refrigeration.

Great resistance to refrigeration is always, as before stated, peculiar to the early stages of the fever, say from the fourth to about the tenth day; in a minor degree it is by no means uncommon. Consequently, the duration of the baths, and in marked cases their temperature, will vary considerably throughout the course of the fever. At the beginning, and to the middle of the second week or thereabouts, they are quite cold, reduced with ice if necessary and of considerable duration ; towards the end, they may be tepid if desired, and need not occupy more than a few minutes.

Some variation in the duration of the baths is also made in accordance with the tendency which all cases present to remit and exacerbate at certain periods of the day.

In all cases with intense and obstinate temperatures, it is necessary to watch carefully the period of ascent, for, as already stated, such patients tend to re-accumulate their fever-heat with great rapidity. Thermometric observations therefore should be taken every two hours, and if the temperature be found as high, or almost as high, as before the last bath, then the bathing should be carried out every two hours. It is very fortunate that these cases, which so urgently demand and so greatly benefit by severe refrigerative measures, are those which pre-eminently support them well. Great obstinacy of the temperature, though possibly not directly due to, is almost always associated with a satisfactory state of the heart and circulation generally; and therefore no hesitation need be felt in pushing the antipyresis with vigour.

It might almost have been assumed that, in the case of children, very obstinate temperatures, even in cases of intense fever, are never met with. It is necessary therefore to proceed with extreme care, beginning with short tepid baths, and gradually prolonging their duration or reducing their temperature, until the desired reduction is attained. Neglect of this precaution might, especially in the case of young children, lead to collapse. The question as to whether it is better to give very short cold baths (three to eight minutes), or tepid baths of longer duration, is an open one. Personally I have a bias in favour of the latter, since children are easily terrified by the shock of cold immersion.

This consideration, however, need not prevent recourse to the former when it is especially indicated by a state of stupor, since the mental indifference then present exercises to a great extent a protective influence, and prevents too great severity of shock.

There is one other danger in the case of young children which seems to me not undeserving of notice. To those who have seen small children bathed in the ordinary full-sized baths, it will not be inconceivable that under certain conditions, *e. g.* inattention on the part of the nurse *plus* great weakness and stupor on the part of the patient, a case of drowning might possibly occur. It would be advisable therefore, where many children are being treated, to have specially-constructed baths of small size. The temperature, however, in young children is usually so amenable to external refrigeration that it is probably better as a rule simply to bathe them in bed, upon a large piece of mackintosh sheeting.

The State of the Circulation

This may call for certain modifications in and additions to the usual treatment. It will have been gathered that the ideal treatment of circulatory feebleness is by prophylaxis, and that this resolves itself into the treatment of the temperature. Systematic refrigeration should be commenced from the earliest possible time; its degree should be apportioned to the intensity of the temperature, and its frequency to the rapidity with which the temperature re-ascends. In the great majority of cases nothing further is required; but there will always, in hospital-practice at any rate, be a residuum in which special treatment is necessary. The residuum comprises—(1) cases which do not come under treatment until late in the disease, and where signs of circulatory feeble-ness are already present; and (2) a very few in which enfeeblement of the circulation has arisen in spite of proper antipyretic treatment from the commencement.

In both classes alcohol is certainly of great use, and no better rules for its administration have been formulated than those of Murchison.

A great variety of drugs have also been recom-mended; among them ammonia, ether, camphor, musk, castor, ergot, cocaine, caffeine, and digitalis. Their number and diversity seem to point to their uselessness. The last alone was found at Brisbane to give appreciable results; it was not, however, used to any great extent, and for the following reasons.[1]

So long as the temperature remains at all high

---

[1] This peculiarity in the action of digitalis was pointed out by Wilson Fox in his clinical lectures.

the drug exerts no influence whatever on the pulse-rate. But should the temperature suddenly fall, the cumulative action of the drug immediately appears; and this happens whether the fall be a natural one, such as occurs at a crisis of the fever or at the onset of intestinal hæmorrhage, or whether it be artificially induced by cold-bathing or an antipyretic drug. In one patient, who was taking 20 minims of the tincture every three or four hours, the pulse-rate ranged from 140 before bathing to 70 afterwards.

There are, however, two drugs which are of decided value as heart-tonics or stimulants in fever, namely quinine and strychnine. The latter is of comparatively recent introduction. It is best given by the hypodermic method, and is especially useful in an emergency and when a rapid reaction is called for. The use of quinine as a heart-stimulant in the Brisbane Hospital dates from the time (1886) when large doses (40 to 60 grs.) were used for their antipyretic effect. In accordance with the more or less prolonged antipyretic action of the doses, there occurred a corresponding diminution in the frequency of the pulse. After a time, however, it was observed that, although the pulse-rate rose with the returning temperature, it usually failed to attain its previous frequency, even when the latter had mounted to an even higher level than at first.

Full confirmation of this fact was obtained on revising the charts of former cases, where it was found that the administration of quinine had almost invariably been followed by a diminished range in the pulse-rate, of longer duration than could be accounted for by the antipyresis obtained.

In addition to the reduction in rate, a decided alteration in character was now observed; a pulse which had been small, soft, and inclined to run, becoming fuller, more forcible, and more distinct. And all these signs of an improved circulation were more marked where the drug had been repeated.

The conclusion that quinine is capable of exerting in typhoid a direct tonic action on the heart, independent of its antipyretic action, is in conflict with the opinion of Liebermeister. Nevertheless it was determined to try the effect of small doses frequently repeated, doses that would not appreciably affect the temperature; and it was found that all the advantages, so far as the circulation was concerned, were to be obtained in this way.

Some peculiarities in its mode of action should be noted. In the first place, the slowing of the pulse-rate is late in appearing, twenty-four hours usually elapsing before it is distinctly perceptible. On the other hand, the effect when obtained is somewhat permanent, for if the drug be suddenly withheld, the

157

pulse does not attain its previous range for some days. This is in contrast to the action of quinine upon the temperature, which is not prolonged for more than thirty-six hours by even the largest antipyretic dose.

The stimulant action on the circulation is much better marked in cases where the feebleness has not reached a high grade. It is therefore in the treatment of *commencing* heart-failure that quinine finds its greatest utility.

A pulse of 120 has usually been regarded as on the border-line between safety and danger, and accordingly a fairly definite rule for the administration of quinine evolved itself. Directly the pulse commenced to attain this rate, three grains of the drug were given every three hours day and night. If no effect was produced in twenty-four hours, the dose was increased to five grains or even to seven grains, though the latter was but rarely required.

It would be easy to quote cases treated in this way in which the ensuing fall in the pulse-rate was plainly visible on the chart. But such evidence would not be of conclusive value, since the pulse-rate in typhoid is notoriously variable under any conditions. Better proof of the value of the drug in sustaining the force of the circulation is obtained by observing the extent to which heart-failure as a cause of death was eliminated from a series of cases, systematically submitted to the operation of the above rule.

The cases admitted during the last eight and a half months of the year 1889 at the Brisbane Hospital constitute such a series. Excluding febricula, abortive cases that convalesced before the tenth day, and all cases not convalescent on December 31, 306 were so treated. Of these eighteen died, a general mortality of 6 per cent.; but of the eighteen fatal cases, eleven were from perforation, two from hæmorrhage, and three from dysentery. In the last case extensive ulceration of the rectum was disclosed *post mortem*, so that in sixteen the fatal result was directly due to the intestinal lesion. Of the remaining two, one was from pneumonia. Up to within twenty-four hours of the termination of this case, no sign of cardiac failure had shown itself; when suddenly pneumonia, involving the whole of the left lung and a great portion of the right, set in with such intensity that the patient succumbed apparently to a mixture of syncope and collapse. There was literally no time to obtain the effect of any drug; so rapid was the failure that at the post-mortem examination the lungs were found to be still in the first stage of a croupous pneumonia, heavy, engorged, but with no trace of true hepatisation. In the last case the exact cause of death remained uncertain. The patient, a young girl, had completely convalesced, and had been in fact allowed to get up. Suddenly, however, she was seized with high temperature, a painful inflammatory swelling appeared in the right submaxillary gland, and she rapidly died with hyperpyrexia. The girl had been suffering from sore fingers, and it was suggested that death was due to septicæmia contracted from a case of puerperal fever occupying an adjoining bed. Be that as it may, the analysis of the eighteen fatal cases shows that during the period in which quinine was given systematically in addition to the cold-bathing, no case out of the 306 treated succumbed to the usual form of cardiac failure, which is admittedly under ordinary treatment the most frequent mode of death.

In attributing this to the combined result of cold-bathing and quinine, one reservation must be made. In every case where the latter was used, alcohol in small doses was also given. But these are the cases in which alcohol has always been administered, without, however, producing any such marked influence upon the pyrexial death-rate. One thing is certain, that the use of quinine, in the manner indicated, has greatly economised the consumption of alcohol in the Fever-wards, more than four ounces in the twenty-four hours being quite exceptional.

A very advanced degree of cardiac feebleness is usually cited as one of the contra-indications to the employment of the cold bath. Some authorities cease bathing altogether under these conditions; others advise that the baths be given tepid, or warm and gradually cooled down with ice, after the manner of Ziemssen. The object of course is to avoid shock, which might in the enfeebled state of the circulation cause a sudden syncope. The danger certainly seems a rational one *à priori*, but I must say that personally I have never seen a single instance of syncope or collapse from the use of the cold bath. But, as already mentioned, the water in Brisbane is usually at 75° F. or more, and this might be held to account for the absence of these accidents. I would certainly hesitate to use water at 68° in these cases, more especially as this can never be necessary; for where feebleness of the circulation is a prominent feature of the patient's condition, the temperature is always easily reducible. Baths of a temperature of 80° F. are quite sufficient in the vast majority of cases, and such baths are never accompanied by symptoms of shock. These patients are all of course taking alcohol in some form, and it is as well to follow the general rule and administer a portion of it immediately before each bath.

This is probably the best place to allude shortly

to the treatment of typhoid in aged persons. In them, as a rule, pyrexia is but moderate and is easily reduced ; but there is, on the other hand, a special tendency towards early adynamia and heart-failure. Vigorous antipyresis is therefore contra-indicated as a rule, while tepid baths of comparatively short duration are found to be both efficient and grateful to the patient. Of course the special tendency to cardiac weakness requires an early recourse to alcoholic stimulants and quinine, while strong beef-tea or other meat-extracts have seemed to be especially beneficial.

Respiratory Symptoms and Complications

The efficient prophylactic power of cold-bathing against the common chest-complications of typhoid has already been referred to. It is necessary, however, to consider the modifications that may be required when such complications are actually present, whether they have been existent on admission or have arisen in spite of the treatment.

The initial slight bronchial catarrh has been shown to be most favourably influenced by cold-bathing ; consequently it calls for no modifications. Indeed it constitutes an extra indication, were any required, for continuing the treatment with vigour and regularity. When this is done, the catarrh passes off long before the termination of the fever, and only in rare instances does any kind of pneumonia develop.

With broncho-pneumonia, however, it is different. Were it indeed necessary to consider the lung-lesion only, no difficulty would arise; its onset would but add to the indications for cold-bathing. But here the condition of the circulation is of paramount consideration. Broncho-pneumonia is invariably a late complication; when present on admission, and still more when it has arisen in spite of systematic refrigeration from an early period, it is always accompanied by a certain degree of cardiac failure, if indeed the latter is not a prime factor in its causation. It is safer therefore to allow the state of the circulation to point out the kind and amount of refrigeration to be employed, and to ignore the pulmonary lesion. The treatment in fact simply resolves itself into the treatment of cardiac failure, concerning which enough has already been said.

Lobar pneumonia may supervene at any period. When limited in amount and early in its onset, it does not necessarily imply any marked deterioration in the quality of the pulse, and therefore calls for no modification in the treatment. But when it supervenes at a later period, or when a large extent of lung-tissue is involved, rapid cardiac failure is to be expected. Here again then the state of the

163

circulation must be allowed to determine the kind of antipyretic treatment to be adopted.

Hypostatic pneumonia may be regarded simply as a part of the typhoid state, and requires no special consideration.

The special treatment of secondary pneumonia by expectorant drugs, stimulating or otherwise, local applications such as poultices, cold compresses, ice-bags, etc., was long ago abandoned in the Fever-wards of the Brisbane Hospital. The distress and irritation caused by the employment of the latter seemed to call for more definite evidence of their utility than was forthcoming.

Nervous and Psychical Symptoms

These have been shown to be on the whole more rapidly and favourably affected than any other group of symptoms; it follows therefore that in most cases but little modification in the general rule of bathing is required. Still, since it has been demonstrated that baths of different temperatures and different modes of application have different effects upon the nervous system, it would be irrational to ignore this fact altogether in the treatment.

In all cases the head and face should be freely bathed before the rest of the body is submerged, and it is preferable to use for this purpose water of a lower temperature than that of the bath. More particularly is this essential when headache is already present, as neglect of this precaution can hardly fail to intensify the symptom.

Generally speaking, the treatment of mental disturbance will vary according as the predominant features are those of excitement or the reverse. In cases with wild delirium, it is in my opinion better to avoid the shock of sudden cold immersion; tepid baths, gradually reduced by the addition of ice if the temperature is obstinate, and supplemented by cold affusion of the head and neck during immersion, have appeared to give better results. On the other hand, in cases showing a tendency to stupor or coma, the sudden shock of cold immersion is of the greatest value, more so sometimes than the reduction of temperature. Very short and very cold baths have consequently here their greatest utility.

There are, however, certain considerations which in practice detract largely from the value of these maxims. In the first place, cases showing wild delirium are usually in the early stage of the fever, in that stage when the temperature is most difficult to reduce, when it is most necessary to reduce it, and when most is to be gained by its reduction. Consequently the most powerful means of refrigeration, the prolonged cold bath, is imperatively called

THE COLD-BATH TREATMENT OF

for; although it might be true that a tepid bath, in virtue of its more soothing influence, would be more appropriate so far as the nervous condition was concerned. Again, cases in which the mental disturbance assumes the form of stupor or coma are frequently in the last stages of the typhoid state, with rapid fluttering pulse and all the signs of advanced cardiac failure. In this state the temperature is easily reduced, therefore very cold water is unnecessary, and according to most authorities is by no means free from danger.

It will be seen then that the opportunities for employing baths of varying temperature, in accordance with their known physiological actions on the nervous system, do not present themselves as frequently as might at first sight be imagined. For certainly when two indications seem to clash, when, for instance, the temperature and circulation demand one form of antipyretic measure and the nervous symptoms an opposite one, then the former should as a rule be allowed to override the latter. Practically it is found that the larger one's experience of cold-bathing, the more frequently one reverts to the original formula.

One nervous symptom, an intense dread of the bath, is occasionally a source of much trouble. Generally, however, moral suasion, with or without a small dose of alcohol just before the bath, will succeed in overcoming it. In one case in which this utterly failed, and in which it was considered urgently necessary to continue refrigeration, the baths were reduced in frequency, and small hypodermics of morphine were administered shortly before each. The result was a complete success, the whole mental attitude of the patient seeming to change under the influence of the drug. Later on injections of acidulated water were substituted, and no further trouble was experienced.

Reference has already been made to those uncommon cases in which delirium arises during the continuance of cold-bathing or persists in spite of it. Some of these are mild, the delirium being interrupted by periods of sleep; they need no special treatment. When, however, delirium is continuous, and therefore accompanied by insomnia, a very dangerous condition is present which may terminate in rapidly-fatal exhaustion. Special treatment is then urgently called for.

In my hands the administration of narcotic drugs, although it may be the last and only resource, has been singularly unsuccessful. To be effectual they require to be given in somewhat heroic doses, and therefore before resorting to their use other measures should be exhausted. In several cases, enveloping the whole head and nape of the neck in cloths wrung out of hot water has been successful,

167

in one or two almost instantaneously so. In other cases, where the temperature has been continuous and obstinate, and where as yet no signs of circulatory failure were present, a single moderately large dose (seven or eight grains) of antifebrin has succeeded perfectly, the falling temperature being followed by cessation of the delirium and prolonged sleep.

Urinary Symptoms

Retention of any kind does not *per se* constitute a bar to further bathing. The common form present on admission, and due simply to nervousness, never necessitates the catheter, and can always be overcome by a little resolution on the patient's part. Usually a screen placed round the bed to ensure privacy is all that is required, or it may be necessary to allow the patient to assume the upright position on the first few occasions.

True retention occurs in the later stages of the fever. It is usually accompanied with signs of mental disturbance or commencing paresis, and is to be regarded as one of the features in the typhoid state. In common with the others, it has been almost banished from cases that are bathed systematically from an early period. When present it does not in itself call for suspension of the treatment, although the associated general state may demand some modification therein. For the retention, Jacques' soft india-rubber catheters are most convenient, since they can be used by the wardsman without risk. Several should be kept ready in the ward in a glass jar containing carbolic solution. They should be used rather frequently, so as to avoid any distension of the bladder.

Albuminuria in small quantity, and unaccompanied with casts, calls for no modification of the treatment. When albumin is present in quantity, accompanied by casts, and perhaps with a smoky appearance of the urine, I have been accustomed to regard it as a contra-indication to further bathing. Even on this point, however, there is considerable difference of opinion; fortunately the question is not likely to arise frequently.

Digestive Symptoms: Diarrhœa and Meteorism

Symptoms in connexion with the upper part of the alimentary canal never necessitate any suspension or modification of the ordinary rule of bathing, although, as previously mentioned, dryness of the tongue and mouth may call for its continuance at a time when the temperature has ceased to demand it.

Neither *diarrhœa* nor *meteorism* call for a cessation of the bathing or for any modification of it, always provided the latter be not one of the symptoms of peritonitis. They both, however,

169

demand additional refrigerative measures. Cold-bathing has been shown to exert a most happy effect on both; such treatment, however, is at best but intermittent. In addition it is always advisable to increase and prolong the action of the bath during the interval by local cold applications, of which by far the best is the ice-bag.

The ordinary bags are faulty in shape, being too small and having only one compartment. As a consequence, they cover but a small part of the abdomen, and should the patient lie in any position other than the dorsal, the ice gravitates, and then only a surface still smaller than the bag is refrigerated.

A much better form of ice-bag was made for me by Weiss. It is a large oval, long enough to extend from the ensiform cartilage to the pubes, and sufficiently wide partly to cover each lumbar region. It is divided by vertical partitions into four equal compartments, each compartment communicating with the single central aperture, which is closed by a cap in the ordinary way. The compartments keep the ice equally distributed, so that in whatever position the patient may lie, the whole of the abdominal surface is uniformly refrigerated. When about to be used, each compartment is filled with ice broken into pieces about the size of walnuts. A single layer of lint separates the abdomen from the ice-bag, which is fixed in position by a towel passed round the trunk and secured with safety-pins.

In all cases in which the symptoms of diarrhœa or meteorism are at all prominent, it is well to have the diet at any rate partly predigested. At Brisbane the milk is peptonised with Fairchild's Zymine; the beef-tea is strained of all sediment, and then thickened with Carnrick's Beef-peptonoids.

Under systematic cold-bathing, the constant application of the abdominal ice-bag, *plus* a predigested diet, it is rare for either of these symptoms to cause anxiety. There remain, however, two forms of diarrhœa concerning which such cannot be said—(1) a copious serous diarrhœa, depending on ulceration of the cæcum and colon; and (2) diarrhœa of a dysenteric character, probably always dependent on extension of ulceration into the sigmoid flexure or rectum. The former demands the prompt administration of opium and astringents. I have usually given a mixture containing turpentine in mucilage with laudanum; sometimes sulphate of copper, as recommended by Murchison, has succeeded in severe cases, where everything else has failed. Certainly the sooner this kind of diarrhœa is checked the better, since it has a rapidly-exhausting effect upon the patient, second only to that caused by hæmorrhage.

171

The dysenteric variety nearly always appears late in the disease, frequently indeed after apparent convalescence. During the first three years of the "bath period" it led to fatal exhaustion in nine instances. In all it was preceded by more or less prolonged diarrhœa; in two the preceding diarrhœa gradually took on the dysenteric characters; in the remaining seven there was a distinct interval, the dysentery appearing almost as a sequela.

Personally I have found treatment in the severe forms of this affection very unsatisfactory, although of late I have had some good results by washing out the rectum with copious injections of weak sublimate solution, followed by enemata of starch and opium.

There is one point in the treatment of meteorism that it is of great importance to realise fully, namely, that cases are manageable in inverse proportion to the amount of intestinal distension and to its duration; *slight distension treated at once never gives rise to anxiety*. On the other hand, when this symptom has reached a high grade, and especially when it has persisted for some time, complete success is more doubtful; the distension even when relieved is apt to return at the slightest intermission of the treatment or even without such intermission. Consequently the rule is to apply constantly the ice-bag treatment to every case,

172

immediately it commences to show the slightest indication of tympanites.

Meteorism in certain cases requires additional treatment. When associated with constipation, enemata of turpentine or simply of cold water are very effectual. Sometimes, however, the co-existence of diarrhœa does not contra-indicate the use of enemata. The best results have often followed the combination of opium internally and ice-bags to the abdomen with two or even three turpentine enemata in the twenty-four hours. Frequent changes of position, especially the Sims gynæcological position with the hips raised, often enables the patient to pass flatus, and the passage of a tube into the rectum is at times of benefit.

Finally, there are cases of extreme distension of the colon in which relief can only be obtained by puncture of its transverse portion. These are mainly cases of peritonitis, under which head they are further considered.

Hæmorrhage

The statement, that the occurrence of intestinal *hæmorrhage* contra-indicates further cold-bathing, requires some modification. It is well known that all varieties of this accident are not of equally serious import. Brand distinguishes two varieties —(1) true hæmorrhage, where the blood is in considerable quantities, and where it comes presumably from a vessel of some size; and (2) false hæmorrhage, where it is slight, and is supposed to be due to capillary congestion. He does not consider that the second variety contra-indicates the bath.

As pointed out, however, by Tripier and Bouveret, the quantity of blood voided is no certain guide to the source of the bleeding; copious arterial hæmorrhage being often preceded by slight blood-stains in the motions. They prefer therefore a classification into—(1) early hæmorrhage, appearing before the twelfth day, and (2) late hæmorrhage, which may appear at any time subsequently. Only the first variety do they consider to be no bar to the bath, since they are of opinion that, before the twelfth day, ulceration has not taken place, and therefore no large vessel can be involved.

Of the general truth of this opinion I have no doubt: out of sixty-three cases observed by myself, in fifty-two the hæmorrhage appeared for the first time later than the twelfth day, four on the twelfth day, and seven earlier. Of the four that occurred on the twelfth day, three were very severe, and in two of these the history of the invasion was most definite, leaving no doubt as to the correctness of the date. Of the seven that occurred earlier than the twelfth day, three were on the eleventh, one on the tenth, and one on the ninth; in all of these either the amount lost was slight or the history of the invasion was indefinite. Two cases, however, occurred on the seventh day; in both the history of invasion was definite, and in one the quantity of blood lost was sufficient to reduce the temperature to the normal.

It would seem that the time at which ulceration commences is not so constant as has been supposed. Murchison refers to cases where perforation occurred on the eighth, ninth, eleventh, and twelfth days, and in one of my own cases it occurred in the middle of the twelfth. In the latter case the date of invasion was easy to fix, as the patient went to bed feeling absolutely well, and awoke the following morning with headache, *malaise*, and complete anorexia. If therefore complete perforation can happen in twelve days, it certainly seems probable that sufficient ulceration to lay open a large vessel might occur even earlier. For this reason, then, and considering the extreme difficulty so commonly experienced in fixing the exact date of invasion, great caution should be used in continuing the bath after hæmorrhage of any sort has occurred.

When the invasion has been definite, and the case has not gone beyond the tenth day, hæmorrhage in small amount does not, in my opinion, necessitate suspension of the bathing; if, however, as in the case mentioned above, it is sufficient to affect the temperature, it is better to wait until all trace of blood has disappeared from the stools. On the other hand, when bleeding appears at a later period, or in cases where the invasion has been vague, the baths should be stopped at once, and the proper special treatment immediately adopted; and this whether the hæmorrhage is large in quantity or amounts only to a mere trace.

The only special treatment that has appeared to me to be of any value is that recommended by Broadbent. A full dose of laudanum (40 to 60 minims) is immediately given, and the abdomen covered with a large ice-bag. But little should be given by the mouth, and that little should be completely peptonised, so as to undergo the most complete absorption possible in the stomach. The patient should be confined strictly to the supine position, and carefully watched to ensure his maintaining it. Under these conditions a sacral bedsore often forms with startling rapidity; it should be a rule therefore, to which there should be no exceptions, that he be placed in the first instance, and directly after the first dose of opium, on a water-bed. If the immobilisation is carried out strictly as it should be, no opportunity for examining the sacrum during the next day or two will occur; and the moving necessary for the change of beds will be less likely to induce fresh hæmorrhage during the tendency to syncope that follows the first attack than later, when reaction has set in. Smaller doses of laudanum should be given during the next day or two, with the object of maintaining aperistalsis.

The question next arises, How long, in the event of the bleeding not recurring, is it advisable to wait before recommencing the baths? The answer will depend upon a variety of circumstances. Profuse hæmorrhage always causes a decided drop in the temperature, which, however, is but temporary. In some cases, especially in those that are approaching convalescence, although it rises again past the bathing-point, yet it fails to attain its previous height; and, unless the symptoms of pyrexia assume an urgent form, it may then be as well to discontinue bathing altogether. In other cases, however, and these are the most common, the temperature at its rebound rises to a greater height than before, and as it is now quite uncontrolled, the whole train of well-known pyrexial symptoms, which had previously been suppressed, appear, it may be for the first time in the case. I have frequently seen the whole aspect of a case, in these circumstances, change completely in a couple of days. Previously the patient had practically no symptoms but high temperature, a more or less thickly-coated tongue, and anorexia; two days after the cessation of bathing, necessitated perhaps by a hæmorrhage quite insufficient to be hurtful in itself, he would present the typical old-fashioned picture of typhoid—high fever, delirium, dry brown tongue, sordes, and tremulous muscles; so that no one who had seen him on both occasions could ever again doubt the amazing efficacy of the bath-treatment in averting the typhoid state.

In such cases it is, of course, a question of comparative risks on either side. While waiting until hæmostasis is presumed to be complete, it is better, I think, to control the temperature by a few doses of antifebrin than to leave it absolutely unchecked. Should there be no re-appearance of the hæmorrhage within three days, I have been in the habit of resuming the bath-treatment, and I have seldom had cause to regret this practice. Where the typhoid state becomes very rapidly developed, it may be worth while to consider the advisability of resuming treatment at the end of forty-eight hours; but, of course, each individual case must be dealt with on its merits.

Perforation

The occurrence of *perforation* demands the immediate and permanent suspension of the bath-treatment; thenceforward the pyrexia sinks into insignificance compared with the urgent danger of rapid general septic poisoning. At present it is an open question whether the treatment should be medical or surgical; whether, indeed, laparotomy is justifiable. Systematic bathing, however, has so altered the symptoms of this accident, and rendered so certain the possibility of its immediate diagnosis, that the whole question of treatment requires re-consideration.

Under expectant treatment, the diagnosis is not infrequently impossible at the time. At the Brisbane Hospital, up to the end of 1886, it was not uncommon to discover perforative peritonitis for the first time in the Post-mortem room. Pearce Gould, in opening a discussion on the operative treatment of perforative typhoid ulcer, states that the symptoms of the accident are either—(1) sudden pain and distension of the abdomen, vomiting, rise of temperature and pulse-rate, and all the signs of peritonitis; or (2) quite latent, consisting only in an increase in the prostration, with distended motionless belly, so that the condition is not even suspected.

In contrast to this is the experience of the Brisbane Hospital during the first three years of the bath-treatment. During this time thirty-four cases suffered perforation, *but so clear was the mental condition in all these patients, that in every instance they were able to fix almost exactly the*

179

time of the accident. Not only so, but they were able, as a rule, to give so significant an account of the onset, site, and character of the pain, that usually a positive diagnosis could be made even before the signs of peritonitis were apparent.

Referring to the cases where the onset is sudden and definite, it is not quite accurate to say generally that the symptoms of perforation are sudden pain and distension of the abdomen, vomiting, etc. Such symptoms undoubtedly occur in nearly all cases, but in not a few they come on progressively, not by any means simultaneously, and distinct intervals can be observed between their appearances.

Reference has already been made to the two varieties of perforation, which occur in the early and the late stages of the fever respectively; and it is not going too far to say that the two varieties generally present distinct clinical features. Early perforation, almost of necessity accompanied by sudden and great extravasation of gas and fæcal matter, rapidly leads to collapse, general peritonitis, toxæmia, and death. With perforation occurring in the later stages, it is not necessarily so. The process is then comparatively slow, an advancing zone of inflammatory action precedes the ulceration; peritoneal adhesions, soft and ineffective in the long run it may be, have time to form to some extent before the accident actually happens, and the amount of the fæcal matter effused is, at first at any rate, often very small. Should the bowel at this time be subjected to any sudden strain, rapid effusion of its contents will occur, and the further course of the case will be the same as in the first variety.

These steps in the process are not imaginary, but can frequently be recognised clinically where the patient's mental condition remains clear. A sudden pain, localised in one part of the abdomen, followed in a short time by tenderness and hardness limited to the same area; next an attack of vomiting and increased abdominal pain; and then all the signs of acute general peritonitis.

The immediate increase in the severity of all the symptoms which follows the first attack of vomiting was very frequently noticed, and I think that this is to be explained only by assuming a sudden additional extravasation of bowel-contents. *It is, therefore, of immense importance to anticipate the onset of vomiting.*

For this purpose a full dose of morphine (one-third to one-half grain) is immediately injected, all food and drink are absolutely prohibited, and the patient immobilised on a water-bed. Whether this treatment is to have any chance of success or not will depend upon the time that has elapsed between the perforation and the injection; and this time, be

181

it said, is to be measured in many cases by minutes. So important is the question of time, that in Brisbane the nurse in charge of the Fever-wards was, in certain circumstances, authorised to administer the first injection without waiting for the Resident's visit, and this, I am convinced, determined the recovery from perforation in one of my cases.

Up to this point the medical and surgical treatment of perforation are identical; thence-forward they diverge. The medical treatment is illustrated by the following two cases.

Case 1.—A. W., married woman, aged 29, on the forty-eighth day of the fever, awoke suddenly at a quarter to five a.m., complaining of intense pain in the right iliac region; an immediate hypodermic injection of morphine ($\frac{1}{4}$ gr.) was administered. A few hours later there was marked tenderness, hard-ness, and complete absence of respiratory movement over the seat of pain. The right thigh alone was flexed. In addition the voice was altered in quality, and the pulse, which had previously ranged between 110 and 120, rose to 140, and later to 164, becoming at the same time small and hard. An occasional piece of ice only was allowed by the mouth; peptonised enemata, with brandy, were given every three hours. The patient was kept well under the influence of the morphine, to do

182

which it was found necessary to give one-third grain every two to four hours night and day. This treatment was pursued for three days, at the end of which time a few teaspoonfuls of chicken-broth were allowed by the mouth, and the following day a little iced champagne. Vomiting never occurred, and the symptoms of peritonitis gradually subsided. Seventeen days after the accident she was apparently convalescent, and four days later she was removed to a couch for the first time. Unfortunately, however, later on severe dysenteric diarrhœa set in, and she died greatly emaciated six weeks from the time of the accident. At the autopsy there was found inflammatory redness, with superficial ulceration of the sigmoid flexure. This, no doubt, accounted for the fatal diarrhœa. Just above the ileo-cæcal valve, the ileum, for about two inches of its length, was firmly bound down to the iliac fascia by a mass of adhesions, completely organised. On opening the gut, a small depression was found on the mucous surface, probably corresponding to the perforation, and opposite this the adhesions were especially dense; no sign of peritonitis elsewhere. The scars left by the typhoid ulcers were plainly visible, but the whole mucous surface of the small intestine was otherwise normal.

The next case illustrates some additional points in the treatment of perforation.

Case 2.—Jane C., aged 23, was admitted on the tenth day of the fever. For the next fortnight all the symptoms were very severe, more especially the diarrhœa and meteorism. On the twenty-fourth day perforation occurred at six p.m., as evidenced by the sudden onset of pain in the right iliac region, rapidly followed by tenderness, hardness, and the abolition of respiratory movement over the lower half of the abdomen. The same treatment as in the last case was adopted, nothing whatever being allowed by the mouth. The pulse, however, continued to rise, and the abdomen became greatly distended. Forty-eight hours after the accident, the transverse colon was punctured with the aspirator-needle, and a large quantity of gas allowed to escape. On the following morning the patient's condition was as follows:—Abdomen, and especially the transverse colon, enormously distended; vomiting, or rather regurgitation of liquid and hiccough constant; surface of body covered with cold sweat; face and extremities bluish; pulse small and feeble, about 160 in frequency. The colon was again punctured, this time in two places, and with the happiest results: retching, hiccough, and cold sweats immediately ceased; the normal colour and expression returned to the face, and the pulse fell at least thirty beats a minute, becoming, at the same time, distinctly larger and

184

stronger. During the next two days the colon was punctured many times, in fact, as often as it showed any tendency to distension. Vomiting did not recur, and the symptoms of peritonitis gradually subsided. On the twenty-ninth day of the fever, and the sixth from the time of the accident, they had, in fact, disappeared. The abdomen was soft and free from tenderness; the pulse 112, but large and full; and she was for the first time allowed nourishment by the mouth. Unfortunately, next day she expressed a desire for a bed-pan, which was given her by an inexperienced nurse. During the attempt to use it she was seized for the second time with all the symptoms of perforation. General peritonitis ensued, and she died in thirty-six hours.

At the autopsy the exact seat of the original perforation could not be distinguished owing to the matted condition of the coils of the intestine. It was, however, no difficult task to discriminate between the partially-organised adhesions, the remains of the first attack of peritonitis, and the semi-purulent lymph due to the second. No trace of the punctures could be seen in the colon.

In this case, it seems reasonable to suppose that the patient might have recovered had the action of the bowels been deferred for a few more days, when the adhesions would have been stronger.

Instead of being encouraged, the desire to unload the rectum should have been immediately suppressed by morphine given hypodermically.

Another point of much interest in this case is the direct causal relation between the abdominal distension and the signs of cardiac failure and other serious symptoms. That the alarming condition of the patient was mainly due to the mechanical " crowding " of the heart was placed beyond a doubt by the immediate result of the puncture. Usually, of course, meteorism can be treated by enemata, but when accompanied by peritonitis, in all probability the result of perforation, such measures are inadmissible, since they increase for the time being the strain on the gut. Even the passage of the rectal tube is often enough to induce an action of the bowels, accompanied by a reflex contraction of the abdominal parietes, that is quite sufficient to cause extravasation of the bowel-contents. Under such conditions, then, puncture of the transverse colon is a most valuable method of treatment; it is in point of fact our only safe resource, and though it was frequently used at Brisbane, none but good results ever followed upon it.

There can, however, be little doubt that the treatment of perforation, in hospitals at any rate, will in future be mainly by laparotomy; and

186

that those hospitals in which the routine treatment is by systematic cold-bathing will provide by far the largest supply of *suitable* cases for this operation. It seems to be a general idea that all, or at any rate most, of the subjects of typhoid-perforation are in an advanced state of prostration at the time of the accident. This is unfounded; in perhaps as many cases, indeed, there have been previously no symptoms, abdominal or general, to cause the slightest anxiety ; a moderate degree of pyrexia, anorexia, and a pulse-rate of from 80 to 110, would practically complete the clinical description. Given such a case, in which vomiting has been anticipated, and in which collapse is not marked, it seems to me not only justifiable to operate, but unjustifiable to wait, and I should feel inclined to regard the prognosis of the operation as anything but hopeless.

After the first hypodermic injection has been given, provided of course it has been given sufficiently early, there is usually an interval of perhaps an hour or two, during which the patient does not get rapidly worse; and during this time preparations for immediate laparotomy can be made.

As to the site of the section, it is generally admitted that were it possible to localise the perforation, it would be of advantage to cut down directly over it. This would be especially the case

187

where operation is performed very early, and where probably the peritonitis is still limited to the immediate neighbourhood of the lesion. It is the opinion of many, however, that the position of the pain is no guide to that of the lesion. My own experience leads me to a different conclusion, namely, that in the majority of cases the *locality pointed out by the patient as that in which the pain began* is a very good index of the site of perforation. The only cases where this does not hold good are those in which the pain is referred to the region of the umbilicus. When the pain is reflected at all, it is in my experience to the region of the umbilicus and not elsewhere. Consequently if it is felt elsewhere, then it is not a reflected pain, and the lesion will be found to correspond with its site. But it does not follow that all umbilical pains are reflected. In one of my cases, perforation occurred while I was at the bed-side; the patient pointed out a spot one inch above the umbilicus; this was marked, and found at the necropsy exactly to correspond to the lesion.

If these conclusions are correct, then the rule would be *always to make the section over the part where the pain began;* if this is not umbilical the lesion is more easily reached; if it is umbilical, and the lesion is not found immediately beneath, then more room is obtained for exploration. At any

188

rate, if, as in the majority of cases, the pain starts from the right iliac region, then no hesitation need be felt in placing the incision to that side, since the probability is always in favour of the lesion being found in that direction.

On opening the abdomen, the perforation may not be immediately found, and then it is important to have clear ideas as to the part of the bowel most likely to be affected. In thirty-two autopsies performed by myself, the distance of the perforation from the ileo-cæcal valve was recorded : in fifteen, it was within six inches ; in twelve, between six and twelve inches ; in two, between two and three feet ; in one, four feet ; in one, in the transverse colon ; and in one, in the cæcum. In three of the cases there were two perforations.

I have myself operated only in one instance, and that was in no sense a test case, since general peritonitis, considerable collapse, and fæcal vomiting were already present. But from my experience in this case, and otherwise, I would venture to make the following suggestions :

1. Operate immediately the first injection of morphine has begun to take effect.

2. If vomiting has commenced, wash out the stomach before administering chloroform.

3. When the lesion is found, and distension of the small intestines is present, enlarge the per-

foration longitudinally, both upwards and downwards, and thoroughly drain.

4. Close the opening by a double row of Lembert's sutures.

5. Examine carefully the lower few feet of the ileum to make certain there is no second perforation. There may be found a patch on the point of perforating, which should then be treated as if the accident had actually occurred.

6. Thoroughly flush the peritoneal cavity with hot sterilised water, and place a glass drain-tube as near as possible to the damaged portion of the bowel.

7. The most generally useful incision would be the oblique, slightly-curved incision, recommended for appendix-operations.

There are some considerations which should encourage a more frequent recourse to operation. In many, if not the majority, of abdominal emergencies, there is little to indicate before operation the exact site and nature of the lesion : the diagnosis has to be made after the abdomen is opened ; we may or may not be thoroughly prepared for what is found. In some instances, too, such as perforation of the posterior surface of the stomach, it will be found that the lesion is out of reach, and therefore not amenable to surgical treatment. None of these drawbacks apply to the perforation of typhoid ; the site of the lesion varies but little ; the history leaves, as a rule, no doubt as to its nature ; and from the mechanical point of view at least, it is always easily repaired.

The main obstacle in the way of frequent operation will always be a hesitating diagnosis before the onset of vomiting. Certainly, there are other conditions in typhoid which are at times accompanied by the sudden development of abdominal pain and distension, while tenderness is a sign not always easy to estimate justly. There is one sign, however, which, in my experience, never fails, inasmuch as it is invariable after perforation, but is not exhibited in other conditions, and that is the perfectly characteristic alteration in the rate and quality of the pulse.

INDEX

INDEX

THE END

Richard Clay & Sons, Limited, London & Bungay.

Printed by BoD™in Norderstedt, Germany